Are You
LOSING
CONTROL?

The Common Sense Guide to Parenting
TEENS

by: Carolyn Bergmann

Design by: Glen Erikson

Illustrations by: Irene Stevenson

crackling
communications
www.cracklecom.com

British Columbia, Canada

Crackling Communications
7623 Garfield Drive
North Delta, British Columbia
Canada, V4C 4E6
fax: (604) 594-4553

www.cracklecom.com
email: info@cracklecom.com

Ordering Information:
Please visit the website
or contact the publisher as noted above.

Canadian Cataloguing in Publication Data

Bergmann, Carolyn, 1951-
Are you losing control?

Includes bibliographical references and index.
ISBN 0-9686297-0-9

1. Parent and teenager. 2. Teenagers. I. Title.
HQ799.15.B47 2000 649'.125 C00-910089-X

Printed in Canada

For
Rob and Aaron,
my teachers
and
Steve,
who makes everything possible.

Acknowledgements
My thanks to those who have made this book a reality:
Glen Erikson, who designed this book and dozens of other projects for me, over twenty years of collaboration and friendship; *Irene Stevenson*, an illustrator who has added so much to several of my projects in recent years;
Yolande Burchell, who offered many insights,
and *Keith Pattinson*, who encouraged me more than he realizes, I'm sure, when he kept asking, "When's that book coming out? Parents need it, you know."

Foreword

As a father, grandfather, and professional working with families and young people for over 40 years, I have been subjected to what sometimes seems an unending barrage of what I should learn, understand, or read so that I and other parents can have a better, more satisfying experience raising teenagers. This recommended reading has ranged from theories of adolescent development, to getting tougher, to being more sensitive and permissive, to turning my kids over to professionals, institutions or government who might have a better idea — which my experience indicates they sometimes but too seldom do.

And so I greeted the chance to review *Are You Losing Control? The Common Sense Guide to Parenting Teens* with a degree of skepticism that becomes someone who has been there — both as a parent and through working with countless moms and dads who have participated in *Parents Together*, Boys and Girls Clubs of British Columbia's self-help program designed to assist parents to reduce serious conflict issues with their teens.

I believe *Are You Losing Control?* holds the potential to become one of the most read, dog-eared, and frequently loaned reference that finds itself in the homes of parents seeking advice and ideas that are relevant, practical, and workable. It's not about theory, folks, it's about living and surviving cohabitation with teens. It's respectful to moms, dads, and teens alike and some of the practical advice borders on hilarious — if such a word can ever be appropriately incorporated into the lexicon of parents raising teenagers.

This book will put you in the forefront of awareness about historic modern issues and ideas that affect you and your teens. The chapters entitled Your Changing Role, Values, About Sex, Alcohol and Other Drugs, and Engaging the Adolescent Brain are instructive and fun to read. Those on Keeping Them Safe, Family Transitions, and Older Teens - Young Adults will give readers some maps and routes to choose from as they embark on journeys into separation, divorce, step-families, and boomerang kids.

It's written by a mother who has been there and lived to tell about it, and therein lies much of the value and credibility of this book. As a parent, I've come to believe it is in the fellow travellers among us we will find the humility, honesty, and practical suggestions we need to raise responsible, respectful, and fulfilled young people. Carolyn Bergmann meets that standard for me.

Keith Pattinson
Regional Director,
Boys and Girls Clubs of British Columbia

Table of Contents

Professional Advice
Readers are advised that this book is written
from the perspective of offering the common
sense advice one parent gives another.
Ms. Bergmann is not a licensed professional
counsellor or therapist and urges parents
who believe they need it, to seek the advice
and counsel of professionals.

LOSING CONTROL?

If it feels like you are losing control of your teen, you are.

Taking control of their own lives is the most important developmental task our kids work on during their teen years. If this "work" makes it seem like your home has become a battle zone, your family is not unusual. A teen's push for independence runs smack up against a parent's need to protect them and protecting our kids is a role most of us have gotten pretty good at. If we hadn't, they wouldn't have made it from infancy to adolescence!

Imagine for a moment, however, what it would be like to have a house full of forty-year-old children, still dependant on us to take care of them and make their decisions for them. Makes you shudder, doesn't it? And yet, when we look at how often we try to protect teens from making their own decisions (and learning from their mistakes), a house full of dependant adult children looks exactly like the kind of future we are trying to create.

Losing control of our teens is inevitable – time will see to that. This book is based on the premise that parents will be most effective if they work *with* that inevitability instead of fighting a battle for control that they are certain to lose. There is no law that says parents and teens *must* engage in the power struggles that turn homes into battlegrounds.

Some parents interpret "losing control" to mean that the job of parenting is over and psychologically abandon their teens to figuring out

A teen's push for independence runs smack up against
a parent's need to protect them.

everything for themselves. This approach is just as devastating to the developing adolescent as are power struggles.

While the job of parenting is very different during the teen years, it is the most challenging and exciting parenting most of us will ever do. Our job is far from done!

Your Changing Role

Our children come into the teen years as just that, children. They leave just a few, short years later as adults. The amount of developmental ground they cover in those few years is phenomenal.

Back when they were infants and then children, they looked to us, their parents, for everything they needed to survive: not only food and shelter and love, but to make their decisions for them, set their boundaries, and keep them safe:

How sick is sick enough to go to the doctor?
When is Todd old enough to take the bus by himself?
Does Jaime need a tutor?
How much sleep does a ten-year-old need?

Caring parents answer all these questions and though children might mount campaigns to change the rules, there is security in knowing that someone bigger and smarter than they are is in charge of keeping them safe and healthy. They are generally cooperative most of the time.

Then one morning you ask your sweet-natured child some perfectly reasonable question like, "What are you doing today?" and the response you get back is pure attitude. And you realize ...the hormonal tsunami has beached.

Hormones are like a wake-up call to children. "Hello in there! You're going to be an adult in a few years. You better start taking control of your life now. Up, up, up! Get with the new program already!" Every cell in their body wakes up with a screech and starts straining for independence.

Adolescence is the bridge between childhood and adulthood. As a society we readily acknowledge that it can be a challenging transition. We accept a certain amount of attitude, acting out, and rebellion as normal. We bemusedly tolerate fluorescent hair, body piercing, and eccentric clothing. Most adults don't expect to like or understand teen music, lan-

> ### *Losing control of our teens is inevitable –*
> ### *time will see to that. Parents will be most effective*
> ### *if they work with that inevitability.*

guage, or culture. Adolescent angst is regarded as normal. It's all part of the passage to adulthood and we're confident they will "grow out of it". We did.

What *isn't* acknowledged, however, is that just as teens go through tremendous developmental changes, so too do their parents. Parenting a teen isn't anything like parenting a child. Too often parents don't see the change and try to continue parenting as if the adolescent were just a bigger ten-year-old whom they can still control. But it doesn't work very well. These are the homes where everyone is at war with each other. There is a lot of yelling, door slamming and unhappiness. These families, in which parents and teens are in constant conflict with each other, are in real pain. They are also in real danger of doing so much damage to each other that their relationships may never be repaired.

It's the Grand Prix of parenting and we're in the front seat.

Is all this conflict necessary?

No.

Teens and parents do not have to engage in these out-and-out power struggles. As a society we seem to have accepted this level of conflict between parents and teens as "normal". Many people believe that it's an inevitable stage of family life. But it isn't. It is possible to have a good relationship with our teens and while that relationship will never be conflict-free, the teen years can be the most interesting and fulfilling years of parenting. But parenting teens does require a literal shift in style from protector/teacher to guide. And it's not a shift we make once.

I liken parenting teens to Mauii's famous Road to Hana. This road has hundreds of hairpin turns and, when I was there, my car had a standard transmission. I must have shifted gears a thousand times in the two-to-three hour trip. Why go? Why take a road that requires that much work to drive? Because the views are literally breathtaking. Every turn opens up to another vision of nature that just blows you away. It's worth every one of those shifts.

Parenting teens is like that. Their hormones surge and ebb, some-times within minutes, and we never know what or *who* we're going to be dealing with. No single strategy will work all the time and we need to think on our feet. But there is nothing more exhilarating than watching a teen, gawky with adolescent angst, evolve into a self-confident, emo-tionally healthy young adult. It's the Grand Prix of parenting and we're in the front seat. I can't imagine a more interesting or important place for an involved parent to be.

Nobody's perfect, we all make mistakes. Fortunately, parent/child ties are long-term and durable. These relationships start before the children are born and continue to affect them, even after their parents die. Parents are the most important people in a child's life and, while that may not translate into teens wanting to hang out with us on Saturday night, we are their number one long-term influence.

In parenting our infants and children, many of us lean on our own upbringing for the cues we need to tell us when to feed or cuddle or dis-cipline our children. We are "parenting by instinct", really, parenting according to our own memories of how *we* were parented. We do a lot our parenting on auto pilot, handling things, for the most part, as our parents did.

When it comes to parenting our teens, however, many of us remem-ber our own adolescence as a time when relationships with parents were strained and difficult. Adults *expected* us to rebel and behave badly so they "put their foot down" and did everything they could to control us. We pushed, they pulled. We left home at the earliest opportunity, deter-mined to "get out of there".

Many of us long for a better relationship with our own kids. We are looking for a different model of how to raise our teens and, perhaps for the first time in our parenting history, are recognizing the need to really think through our parenting decisions.

This book offers a new way of looking at your relationship with your teen – mutual respect and affection and the room your teen needs to grow into a healthy, happy adult who makes good and responsible deci-sions for him or herself. Losing control of your teen *is* inevitable. In this book you will learn how to work with that, helping your teen develop the tools and skills he or she will need to make that transition to total con-trol of his or her own life, healthy and well.

Losing control of your teen is inevitable. Work with it.

Chapter One

YOUR CHANGING ROLE

What Will You Need?

A man who was retiring after thirty-five years as a counsellor in a juvenile detention centre was asked what advice he could give parents. What would keep their kids out of such facilities? He reflected for just a moment, then replied, "I've never had a kid in here whose parents were genuinely happy people themselves."

To be really good at parenting teens you need to look after yourself first.

What makes you deep down, genuinely, happy? What gives you satisfaction and pleasure and leaves you feeling refreshed? Make time for those activities and relationships that do that for you. Take care of your own physical, emotional and spiritual well-being first, because parenting teens is intensive and, often, exhausting. You cannot give what you do not have.

Get more selfish about your own needs. Parenting small children is basically a twenty-four-hour-a-day act of self-sacrifice. You may not have realized that with your kids growing up and getting more independent you don't have to do that anymore. Take time and space for yourself now. Serve notice that on Thursday nights from nine-to-ten o'clock the family room television will be on *your* program. From time to time, cook food that you alone like. Reserve some of the family income for your own needs. Buy a ticket to the symphony, a video only you want to watch, a weight-

You cannot give what you do not have.

*No, there is no money for the concert tickets and yes, Mom
just signed up for scuba lessons. Make no apologies.*

room pass, some new clothes, or a painting you love. Dye your hair, take
up scuba diving, join a literary club, learn how to ride a motorbike, buy
a subscription to *People* magazine, or get a make-over.

Kids are accustomed to having all their "needs" met first and will no
doubt be seriously perturbed when you tell them that, "no," there is no
money for the concert tickets they want. And "yes," it is true that Mom just
signed up for scuba lessons, that's why there's no money for their concert
tickets. Make no apologies.

By setting the example of
living well, we show them how to do it.

At first this will be very hard to do. Most of us are so fixed into the groove of denying ourselves for the sake of our children that it's a very hard pattern to break out of. But teens' desire for independence has real benefits for parents. Taking control of their own lives (which they're all in favour of) includes, for example, taking responsibility for their own expenses and they can start with the luxuries of life like concert tickets.

The point is, you have a life too and you need to carve out the time, space, and finances to meet your own needs. Teens pay great lip service to this concept. What parent hasn't been told to "get a life"? But, the developmental stage teens are in makes them so self-centred, they don't really mean it. Sure, they want you to stop running their life, but at the same time, they want you to keep making *their* needs and *their* desires (for money, laundry services, food, and so on) the top priority.

So, expect your teens to get hysterical when you choose scuba lessons for yourself over concert tickets for them; but stick up for yourself. You too, deserve a fair share of the family resources and, if you are like most parents, you haven't been taking your share for years.

You may feel a little selfish doing this, but there are several reasons why it's important:

You Need to Be in Top Form for the Job
First of all, as already mentioned, parenting teens is stressful and exhausting. To do a good job, you genuinely need to be in top form and the activities and experiences and relationships that do that for you are essential. Teens need a lot of love, support, and wisdom. You cannot give this if you are empty, exhausted, and feeling deprived.

You Need a Life
Second, as children grow older, they spend more and more time away from us. They get ever more involved in activities and relationships outside the home and, especially once they or their

friends start driving, need increasingly less of our physical attention. This is the natural order of life. If you've been a real hands-on parent, however, this leaves some major gaps in your lifestyle. You need a life of your own.

Start picking up the pieces of the life you left behind when they arrived as infants and demanded your whole attention. Clean up your golf clubs, re-string your guitar, buy some new paints, volunteer for something, or join a club.

For better or for worse, we are our kids' role models and living a fulfilling, happy, and balanced life ourselves is one of the most important messages we can send them. By setting the example of living well, we show them how to do it.

Everyone's Needs Are Respected

Finally, we need to carve out time and space and money for our own needs because we want our kids to grow up to be caring, thoughtful adults. In fact, on the days when our teen is behaving most selfishly, this promise of a future relationship with a warm, loving adult child is the carrot that keeps us plodding along. Well, caring, thoughtful adults don't just suddenly pop out of birthday cakes at age twenty or thirty or even forty. They become that way when their parents firmly and repeatedly demonstrate that *everyone* has needs that must be respected.

Teens are naturally self-centred because of where they are in their development as human beings. They have so much to sort out – physically, mentally, and emotionally, that they *need* to focus inwardly at this stage in their lives. As they grow older, however, and find answers to big questions like who they are and what they will be, they will begin to look outward again and start taking other's needs into account. As parents we encourage this development along by gently but firmly insisting on having our own needs respected too.

Only you can define, for yourself, what your needs are, but they might include things like: a smoke, alcohol, drug-free home; respectful language; privacy; not having your belongings such as tools, books, or clothes used without your permission; a good night's sleep; a share of the family income for your personal needs and so on. Teens are very big on the concept of having *their* needs and person respected, so you wouldn't think they'd have too much trouble making the leap to respecting their parents needs and person too, but this doesn't seem to happen naturally. Parents need to be assertive about expecting this respect.

And *yes*, teens will act like the sky is falling, but go with it anyway. They really need reminders to look outside themselves and consider others.

> *Parenting is part of our own growing-up process too and parenting a teen is a big step in this evolution.*

GROWING UP

We, ourselves, were infants, toddlers, preschoolers, school kids, teens, and young adults; then, *parents* of infants, toddlers, preschoolers, and so on. Parenting is part of our own growing-up process too and parenting a teen is a big step in this evolution.

Thinking Things Through

We need to work on ourselves, thinking through the issues that will be coming up, ahead of what our kids need.

For example: use of drugs. Sure, most of us will agree that we don't want our kids on crack, but what about the softer drugs like alcohol and marijuana? What's your position? How will you respond when your daughter says, "Hey, Dad, you grew up in the 60s, did you smoke dope?"

You need to think through and, if you have a partner, talk through your feelings about the issues that will be coming up, before they come up. You also need to sort out any major differences between your views and those of your partner.

For Example: Jon believes that it's inevitable that kids are going to drink, so if that's the case, they might as well drink at home where they're safe and he can keep an eye on them. His partner, Sheila, believes this is encouraging the kids to drink and, having grown up in an alcoholic home, she's dead set against the kids drinking anywhere.

How do you recognize unresolved issues of your own?
When you have a powerful, even physical reaction to
something that is out of proportion to the circumstance.

Obviously, differences need to be sorted out by parents, in private, when they are feeling calm and rational. Coming home to find your kids and their friends drunk in the basement is not the time to discover that you hold vastly different views from your partner. It's also worth mentioning that teens are very eager to become adults and will emulate behaviours that they believe are "adult". Telling your kids not to drink alcohol, for example, because it's "only for adults" may do more to encourage this activity than discourage it. You're going to have to come up with more carefully thought-through reasons. The other factor, of course, is our own behaviour. If drinking alcohol is a normal part of our lifestyle we're not likely to have much moral weight to throw around in this area. See *Chapter Four* for much more discussion about communicating values to teens.

Unresolved Issues

Teens often trigger unresolved issues from our own adolescence, and these issues significantly influence our parenting.

For Example: Despite trying out every year, Paul never quite made it onto the basketball team. He was just too short to make it past the big guys and he's never forgotten the humiliation of being passed over because of his size. When his son Josh shot past the six-foot mark by age fourteen Paul was ecstatic. But Josh doesn't want to play basketball and the harder Paul pushes, the more resistant Josh becomes. Lately they've gone days at a time without talking.

For Example: At age fifteen, Louise was nearly raped in the stairwell at a school dance. She looks at her beautiful young daughter and cannot bring herself to allow Alanna to go to school dances. This issue is becoming a major cause of conflict between them and Louise is suspicious that, lately, Alanna has been sneaking out of the house to go to dances anyway.

If we carry baggage from our adolescence (and who doesn't) we need to pull it out and unpack it ourselves. This is not our children's burden. How do you recognize unresolved issues of your own? When you have a powerful, even physical reaction to something that is out of proportion to the circumstance, chances are good that your own unresolved issue has been triggered.

For Example: When Alanna asks to go to a dance, Louise feels her heart start to beat too fast and her stomach churns in anxiety. When Jeff sees the announcements for basketball games at his son's school, he feels angry.

These responses are out of sync, or out of proportion to what they logically should be and a clear sign that Jeff and Louise have something to work out for themselves. Our own issues must not become our children's burdens.

Conflicts With Our Own Parents

Sometimes, a simple physical resemblance or characteristic can resurrect the conflict we had with a parent ourselves and re-visit that same emotion on our relationship with our teens.

For Example: Moira's father believed that something could always be done better. Moira experienced this belief of his as a constant barrage of criticism and it made her defensive and angry around her father. She was determined never to do this to her own kids, and she hasn't, but she finds that she is edgy and impatient with her son Jared. Sometimes, he just makes her so crazy. The pitch of his voice and the way he moves his hands ...he reminds her so much of her own father.

Divorced parents often report this same struggle, when they see a physical similarity or characteristic of an ex-spouse reflected by their teen. It can be very challenging to handle the emotions that this reflection stimulates. Be aware of what is actually fuelling these feelings and

*Family life is bracketed, if you will, by
the adults involved and it is within this
context that teens develop from
children to adults.*

remind yourself that *this* is not your ex-spouse, but your own child, whose character has no doubt been greatly improved by your own genetic contribution!

Look for Help

Just as your child has never been a teen before, you've never been the parent of a teen before. If you are already involved in serious conflict with your teen, reach out for help. Talk to friends and family who have teens of their own, read books, or join a parent support group. Such groups can make a real difference in your life. The parents you meet in a support group have a genuine understanding of what you're going through. They've been there too and can offer empathy, support, some good ideas to work with, and, most importantly perhaps, the knowledge that you're not alone.

PARENT TO PARENT

The parents' relationship with each other, with new partners, or both, is the foundation of their family, whatever its configuration. Nuclear families, stepfamilies, same-sex families, separated families ...in all of them, the relationship of the adults is the foundation on which the family is built and its stability/instability is a major influence on the children. Even if the couple is estranged and live apart, the way those adults interact has an impact on their kids.

For better or for worse, the parent's behaviour is the model that their children observe firsthand. It's where they learn how to resolve conflict (or bury it), how to communicate (or misunderstand), how to show love and affection (or ignore each other), and how to respect each other's needs (or be self-centred).

Family life is bracketed, if you will, by the adults involved and it is within this context that teens develop from children to adults.

Our children learn much more from the example we live out in front of them, than they do from the words that come out of our mouths. How we live out our couple relationship, whether married and living in the same house or divorced and a continent apart, teaches our children how to conduct their own relationships. And it's important to realize that the test of whether we're providing a good model for our kids is not determined by the structure of our relationship with their other parent. Many couples, sleeping in the same bed, year after year, are living a life of veiled animosity and anger. They loathe each other and the kids know it. Another couple may be divorced, but based on their love for their children have managed to work out a co-parenting relationship for their kids that exemplifies respect for each other.

Kids also put a lot of energy into trying to patch up and hold together shaky parent relationships, energy they need to be putting into their own growth and development.

> *Many counsellors will tell you that when a troubled teen is hauled into their office, the first place they look is the parent's relationship.*

For a teen to make a healthy transition from childhood to adulthood, they need to accomplish major developmental tasks. Not everyone completes this work, which is why so many adults are developmentally stuck in adolescence: people who've never found what they want to do with their lives; who don't know what they believe in; who adopt the values of whomever they last listened to; who are insecure about their own sexuality; and who don't have faith in themselves.

Teens who are preoccupied with trying to fix their parent's relationship and who stay awake nights worrying that their family is going to break up aren't doing the developmental work they need to be doing and end up stuck somewhere along the way.

Chronic, ongoing conflict between parents results in emotionally troubled kids who are particularly vulnerable to experiencing depression, withdrawal, poor grades, aggression, rebelliousness, delinquency, and low self-esteem.

Many counsellors will tell you that when a troubled teen is hauled into their office, the first place they look is the parent's relationship. So, yes, the parental relationship does have an enormous effect on the well-being of the kids.

Modelling a Healthy Relationship

This means that couples who are planning to stay together do everything they can to make their relationship healthy and fulfilling. If there are weaknesses in the relationship, they work on them. There are courses, counsellors, weekend encounters, books, videos and support groups all waiting to be accessed. Parenting teens is stressful and it will put added strain on parental relationships. Make sure yours has the reinforcement it needs.

Couples who are fighting and unsure of which way they are headed need to find a mediator to help them sort out their feelings and make some decisions. If they choose to stay together, they need to work on the areas of conflict; there are plenty of counsellors waiting to help them. If the cost of counselling seems too high, remember that it's peanuts next to the cost of maintaining two households.

If the cost of counselling seems too high, remember that it's peanuts next to the cost of maintaining two households.

Explain to the kids that the problems between the adults are just that, between the adults. These problems are not caused by them and cannot be solved by them. While this may make them feel helpless in the face of a storm that may irrevocably change their lives, it also relieves them of the responsibility to save their parent's marriage – a burden too many children stumble under.

If separation and/or divorce are the next step, read *Chapter Twelve* for information about parenting teens through this transition. There is lots parents can do to steer their kids safely through divorce.

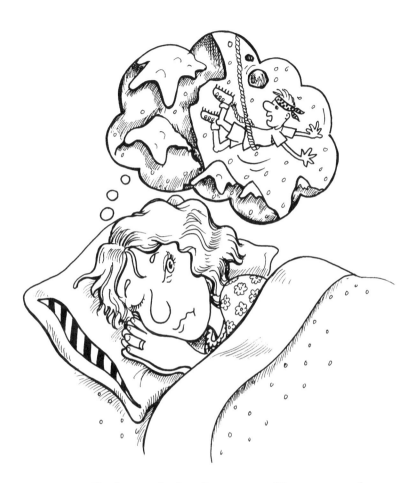

I've learned a lot about controlling my own fear.

THE OPPORTUNITY OF A LIFETIME!

Sadly, parents often think of adolescence as a period in family life that must simply be endured. In fact, the teen years can be both the most interesting years and also, a real catalyst for growth in their parents. When your teen questions your values and beliefs, accept the challenge and use the opportunity to examine them. Many of us find that these years, while our teens are doing so much developmental work of their own, have led us into taking some leaps in maturity ourselves.

Adolescence is a time when our kids are actively exploring who they really are and that makes them interesting and stimulating people to be around. One of my sons developed a passion for climbing and mountaineering when he was a young teen. Because of this we learned a great deal more about rock faces, ice falls, and the world of high altitude climbing than we would have without the stimulus of his participation in the sport. I've also learned a lot about controlling fear and worry and how to sleep soundly in my own bed when I know my son is dangling off the side of some mountain in a sub-zero howling snowstorm!

His quest for the leanest, strongest body possible also revolutionized the family's eating and exercise habits. As we watched his body lean out and grow stronger month after month, year after year, we were motivated to begin making changes in our own lives as well.

My second son is an artist and among the many things he's taught me is an appreciation for graffiti as an art form. Under his tutelage I've learned to recognized the mark that specific artists place on their pieces and to look for these marks. Where I once saw only "defacement", I now see artistic expression. This son is also an adventurous explorer in the world of ethnic cooking and has introduced us to many foods we'd not otherwise have tried. A relentless lacrosse player, he cracked open the locker room door for me. Feminist or not, I now have an appreciation for that factor that I can only define as genuine "maleness".

Because of our kids, their father and I have been introduced to people and sports and books and movies and adventures that never would have been a part of our experience without them. They've been our passport into worlds previously unimagined. I remember hearing a co-worker being asked, years ago, if she planned to have children.

"Well, it might be fine for some people, but I need a much broader perspective on life than diapers and dishes," she replied.

I thought that was a pretty ignorant point of view then and after twenty years of childrearing I *know* it's an ignorant answer. Children have opened worlds of ideas and experiences that I know I never would have ventured into on my own. Thinking that children narrow our perspective is so far from the truth and teens, in particular, have so much to offer their parents. To me, they've been the most interesting years of parenting, by far.

~ Chapter Two ~

YOUR CHANGING RELATIONSHIP
What Will Your Teens Need From You?

Far from being a job that is "almost done", the parenting of teens is a challenging and involving pursuit. Your teen will be looking to you for: time and attention, guidance, a place to belong, respect, a sounding board, a role model, and values.

TIME AND ATTENTION

We've all heard the theory that busy parents could give their kids "quality time" at their convenience and that this "quality time" would make up for the fact that the parents were seldom home. We now know that this parenting theory is an unfortunate myth. Kids do need quality time alright, but since their crises and questions don't happen on a schedule, that means we must simply *be* there. We know our sons and daughters well and are capable of picking up the subtle visual or verbal cues that tell us something is wrong, that they may need our help. We also need to be there to celebrate their successes: the news that she finally made the volleyball team or that he aced the math exam.

Teens are often so involved with their peer group that parents think their opinion doesn't matter, but don't believe it. Parents are the most important people in a teen's life and while a temporary tough-kid attitude may mask it, our approval is something they never stop looking for.

Notice not just their successes, but their efforts. If she didn't actually make the volleyball team, notice that she stayed after school every day for a week trying out. We can't "make it better", but we can notice that she's hurting and give her a hug. Just that we noticed and care, makes a difference already.

Sometimes kids act like our interest in them is an intrusion on their privacy. Ignore it. Part of the work of adolescence is to separate from parents and this process is often a case of two steps forward, one step back. Much like a toddler who shrieks, "Do it myself!", then dissolves in tears and needs a snuggle two minutes later, a teen is trying to be brave and "Do it himself." But this is new ground, emotionally, and there'll be times when he over reaches himself. Times when he needs our reassurance that if he didn't make it *this time*, he will the next. That said, remember that "interest" is not the same as interrogation. Interest means *being there*, and indicating a willingness to talk by offering a comment or observation such as, "You've been looking a little down lately." or "All this practising looks like its kicking the stuffing out of you." If all you get back is a grunt or a mumble, that's okay. You've let them know that you've noticed, that you care, and that you're there for them if they decide they need to talk.

Remember that "interest" is not the same as interrogation.

Getting your teen to talk may not be easy. There are always exceptions, but most teens, once deep into the throes of the separation stage of their development, respond to full frontal interrogation with walls of defensiveness you couldn't break through with a nuclear warhead. Just let them know you're interested enough in them to notice things and that you're there if they need you.

One of the saddest pieces of information to come out of research into teen suicide is that, very often, the teens who attempt suicide don't believe that their parents are glad that they're part of the family. It's heartbreaking to know that there are kids who don't feel valued by their parents, but it's important news for parents who do care.

We must let our kids know, every single day, that we are glad they were born and glad that they're in the family. And believe me, it's not enough to just assume that they know this. They don't. Adolescence is the most emotionally insecure period in our lives. What *we* think they believe and what they *should* believe are irrelevant. The only thing that counts is what *they* believe. Ask them:

"Do you know that I am so glad you are my son/daughter?"

"Do you know that I am thankful you are my son/daughter?"

"Do you know that I am so very, very proud to call you my son/daughter?"

"Do you know that I love you?"

Tell them how you feel. Then show them, by making time for them, that they are a priority in your life. They are important to you and you prove it to them by giving them your time and attention. In any home there will be a dozen reasons in any given day to nag your kids about the dishes in the family room, the wet towels on the floor, the car that has no gas, or the lawn that wasn't mowed. Actively look for instances when they are doing something right and comment:

"The cat sure will be glad you cleaned her litter box!"

"I like what you did with your room."

"Thanks for picking up the family room."

"Connie said you're the best babysitter they've ever had."

"I like that song you were playing this morning."

"The dog sure loves it when you take him along for a run."

While we need to work and we need to nurture our own well-being, parenting teens is not something we can do with little bits of leftover time. This is not the time in our lives to take on a job or pur-

We cannot fly into town, interrogate them over dinner, consider it quality time, and think our job is done. There are no shortcuts to parenting a teen.

suit that is going to take us away from home evening after evening after evening. In just a few, short years they will be adults and we will have the rest of our lives to run for political office, win the master's circuit, or get a Ph.D. Teens need their parents to simply be there for them. We cannot fly into town, interrogate them over dinner, consider it quality time, and think our job is done. There are no shortcuts to parenting a teen.

Teens need us to guide them, not carry them around.

GUIDANCE

Teens need us to guide them, not carry them around on a stretcher. We all know forty-year-olds who were, and still are, being carried around on a parental stretcher. They're the people who've never quite found their way in life. They blow off jobs, can't seem to keep a relationship going, are deeply in debt, lose their driver's license, still depend on their parents to bail them out when they really screw up, and expend a lot of wind blaming the system, the government, the boss, their spouse, their parents, the neighbour ...whomever. Everything that's unsatisfactory in their life is always somebody else's fault and they've never figured out that their own happiness is their own responsibility.

We shake our heads and say that these people are really immature and it's true, that's exactly what they are, immature. They have never developed past a certain point. Somewhere along the way their natural urge to take control of their own lives was stifled.

Making mistakes is not what we actually learn from. The learning happens when we have to deal with the consequences of our mistakes.

Teens need to learn how to make good and appropriate decisions for themselves. They can only do that by practising.

Parents often say that they'll give their teen responsibility "when they show they can handle it". But responsibility isn't something that suddenly appears at a certain age. It's learned when teens find themselves on their own, making decisions for which they will take the consequences. It's very hard to watch your teen walking straight into the face of a mistake, but that is how most of us learn best. Mistakes are not evidence of failure, they're just markers along the way. They are how we all learn not to do something and most of us have to learn that for ourselves.

But *making* mistakes is not what we actually learn from. The learning happens when we have to deal with the *consequences* of our mistakes. And we all put a lot of energy into trying to avoid the consequences of our mistakes; it's just human nature. If teens make decisions that have uncomfortable consequences they will try to convince their parents to rescue them. They will do this by blaming someone or something else for the mistake.

> *For Example: If Tamara loans the new sweater she got for her birthday to a friend whom she knows isn't careful with things, chances are good that it will come back damaged. When this happens (and you knew it would) Tamara is devastated. She will expend a lot of energy trying to convince herself and you that she never thought her friend would be careless with the sweater and that she made her friend promise she'd take good care of it. She wants you to rescue her, just this once, by buying her a replacement.*

It is tempting to do so. But if you do, Tamara will learn that if she ignores the little warning messages she gets in her brain (and she had them, that's why she extracted that promise from her friend) it's okay because her Dad will bail her out. She will have missed the whole lesson about how being discriminating about whom you loan your belongings to is part of taking care of them.

In Another Example: Jake, new license in his pocket, was bombing down the freeway when he saw those distinctive flashing lights in his rear view mirror. Sure enough, a $175 speeding ticket was his. "But it wasn't really his fault," he explained, "because he hadn't actually seen a sign posting what the speed limit was and sure, he knows that sign or no sign the legal speed is never more than 100 kmph but the sun was shining, y'know. It's not his fault that auto manufacturers make cars more powerful than the speed limit."

A few weeks later he arrived home very agitated. He'd received another ticket; this time it was $25 for parking in a restricted zone. Before telling his parents about these tickets he worked out rationalizations for them, reasons why it wasn't his fault and he shouldn't have to pay. He "didn't think there was a sign saying he shouldn't park there. There might have been, but it wasn't very big. It wasn't anywhere near his car. Having a restricted zone there was just plain stupid. It just wasn't his fault."

Since Jake was earning less than $80 per week at his part-time job his parents were tempted, just this once, to pay his tickets for him. But Jake needs to really understand that all those regulations he memorized for his driver's test and the signs posted on the roads are not just theory, he has to respect them and obey them, or suffer the legal consequences. Right now, the $200 in fines he'll have to pay is a huge amount of money to him and it will impress these things on his mind. If his parents pay the fines, the experience of getting the tickets will be just a minor blip on his memory. Driving is grown-up business with grown-up sized consequences and tickets are the least of it.

Teens need to learn to take both the short and long-term consequences of what they do into account in their decision making.

For Example: Terry understands that if she doesn't do her math homework and the teacher does a homework check she will lose marks. So she carefully weighs the odds of this happening and makes her decision based on whether or not she figures the teacher will do a homework check. She might even take into account (on the periphery of her thought processes) that if she doesn't practise her math she'll do poorly on the final exam. But it's doubtful that she'll consider how shortchanging the amount of time she spends working on math now, will affect her ability to do well next year or the year after. But math is a cumulative subject, with each new concept building on the one learned before it and failing to become proficient in one area makes it difficult to do well at a later stage. This could have the long-term consequence of making her grades fall just enough to deny her entry to a post-secondary program she really wants to be accepted for five years from now.

Parents are much better at seeing long-term consequences than teens and, without sounding too much like a nag or doomsayer, parents have an important role in this area. The best time to get into this discussion may not be at 11:30 at night, with an hour of math homework still undone, but at other, calmer times, discuss the long-term consequences of decisions with teens. Help them brainstorm potential problem areas and figure out for themselves how a hastily-made decision today can have ramifications years into the future.

For Example: In agreeing to let a friend hide his stash of marijuana in her locker, Jennifer will probably weigh how likely it is that a locker check will be called that week. But will she think through how such a find and subsequent charges for possession might limit her freedom to travel to other countries in the future?

Or that, as in the earlier example, dropping a difficult math course may have the short term consequence of relieving a source of stress for the teen, but it also significantly narrows his future options when many post-secondary programs (from computer science to nursing) require this course.

It is necessary that teens think through and make decisions for themselves, but it is very important that parents be there to help them explore the short- and long-term consequences of their decisions. It's best if the teen comes up with a variety of options and possibilities themselves, but some prompting may be necessary.

Get out a pencil and paper and encourage them to brainstorm their options.

They look in the mirror and see someone who looks like a real dork, and it's true.

Use questions like:
"What other possibilities might there be?"
"What else could you try?"
"What have other people done about this?"
"Do you see any way this could be done differently?"

After brainstorming options, explore the short- and long-term consequences of each of the options. Again, try to have the teen think through most of these. Use questions like:
"What do you think would happen if someone tried this?"
"Do you think this would improve the situation?"
"What could happen tomorrow if you tried this?"
"How could this affect your life in one or two or ten years?"
"Are these results you could live with?"

The objective here is to get the teen thinking in terms of both short- and long-term consequences. When teens brainstorm consequences themselves (rather than listening to you rattle them off while they sit there daydreaming about their date last weekend) they are developing their critical thinking processes and learning the art of making good decisions for themselves.

If you explore all the options and all the consequences with them and they still make a decision that you don't think is in their best interest, back off and let them learn from it. And who knows, you might be wrong. You wouldn't be the first parent to be!

A PLACE THEY BELONG

Perhaps more than at any other time in their lives, teens need unconditional love. In many cases teens go through stages during these years where they look in the mirror and see someone who looks like a real dork, and it's true. They look like someone that only a mother or father could love, so love them!

Make home the one place they belong. Love isn't a bargaining chip or a reward for looking beautiful or getting good marks or excelling on the soccer field or cleaning their room. They're loved simply because they are themselves.

Make one-on-one time for you and your teen on a regular, scheduled basis. Talk about what you would both genuinely enjoy doing together and take time to do it. Jog together, go to the movies, fix up an old car, take tennis lessons, volunteer as a team at your community theatre, buy season's tickets to something, go fishing, make a date to watch a favourite television show every week or go for a hike.

The important thing is that the activity you choose is something you both genuinely enjoy and that this time is reserved for enjoying each other's company. These are not the times to get into areas of disagreement or to teach them some major lessons about how hard life is! If there's something you need to "discuss" with them, do it at another time. This time is just for fun. It's when you make deposits into an emotional bank account of goodwill and good feelings about each other. This bank account is what will carry your relationship through the rougher times when your teen's push for independence runs up against your need to protect them.

One final word, show up at their games, concerts, and ceremonies. They *do* want you there. The video camera may embarrass them, but they want *you* there. Count on it. Show up.

RESPECT

Respect Their Capability

Teens learn so much, so fast that a parent often doesn't realize how capable they've become. I will never forget the pain in Jared's voice when he told me how his father took the family computer off to the repair shop, even though Jared had told him repeatedly that it was a simple problem he could easily fix. "I fix all the computers at school ...way more difficult stuff ...all the teachers turn to me first ...but my Dad doesn't think I know anything."

Computer knowledge is the most common area in which teens frequently surpass their parents, but think about what your teen is most interested in and chances are, they've long ago outstripped your knowledge in that area. Ask them for help and advice first. If you're wary about whether or not they can handle it, err on the side of trusting your teen. It's that important.

Self-confidence and self-esteem are very hard to generate from within ourselves. They are more the result of having other people's confidence in us reflected back onto ourself. If someone else believes you can do it, you're more likely to have confidence that you can do it. And no one is more influential in this role than a parent.

Teens, at a time in their lives when self-confidence is at an all time low, are so hungry for the self-affirmation that comes from being genuinely respected. Parents are in the best position in the world to give it.

Respect Their Agenda

Teens also need to have their agenda and commitments respected and taken seriously. They report that on virtually no notice, parents expect them to cancel plans of their own to fall into line with the parent's plan, whether that be to clean out the basement or join the family for pizza. Ignoring a teen's own agenda is disrespectful.

Teens Are Not Extensions of Us

Further in that vein, a teen isn't our third arm. Rather than demand their help, we need to ask, politely.

> *For Example: Instead of "Get the hammer!" It needs to be, "Could you get me the hammer, please?"*

Your opinion is just one piece of information they have available to help them make the best decision for themselves.

It may seem like irrelevant semantics, but if we ordered friends and strangers around like this they would instantly let us know how inappropriate it was. We express our respect or lack of it for someone by the way we talk to them and teens are very sensitive to the subtleties of language.

Teens also have a need to establish their own body space. Possessive moves from us (like brushing the hair out of their eyes) can be real flashpoints of irritation. They're growing up. They probably like their hair in their eyes. It's *their* hair. Behaviour that would be inappropriate to another adult will seem even more inappropriate to a teen.

Teens are in transition to adulthood and hypersensitive to any motions of non-confidence from us. We need to respect their privacy and right to personal space, just as we want our own respected. It's that simple.

A SOUNDING BOARD

Learn to listen. This doesn't mean we have to agree with everything they say. Listening is just that, listening. If every time they talk to us we follow up with a ten-minute lecturette, they'll stop talking to us.

If you feel you absolutely have to say *something*, try using the phrase "That's an option." It works almost everywhere and doesn't imply either agreement or disagreement. It's neutral and that's where we need to try and stay most of the time.

Teen's don't want us to solve their problems for them and if we don't want them home and helpless at age forty, we better quit trying to solve their problems for them and let them get on with learning how to handle their own lives capably.

Listen to your teens. Sometimes that's all they need, to talk something out, out loud. But if they need some help, show them how to brainstorm their options, and how to review the short- and long-term consequences of each option.

'bed, they're not taught. Live yours and
... teen will know where you stand.

If your teen asks your opinion, give it, but realize it is just that, an opinion. It's just one piece of information they have available to help them make the best decision for themselves. Your opinion is not the Holy Grail. Don't be offended when they don't take your advice. You could be wrong, which is one of the most exciting things about seeing your teen mature into an adult. Somewhere along the way we realize that we don't know what's best for them anymore. They do.

A ROLE MODEL
Get your own head straight about what you believe in, because you will be challenged:
- If you use illegal drugs, you teach that laws don't matter.
- If you smuggle purchases across the border, you are stating that cheating is okay.
- If you always party with a drink in your hand, a teen learns that they need alcohol to have fun.
- If you have sex with multiple partners, your teen won't buy a connection between sex and commitment.
- If you make racist slurs, they'll believe they're true

On the other hand:
- If you genuinely treat all people as equals, they'll assume it's so.
- If you live with integrity and honesty, they'll believe those are the standards everyone should live by.
- If you vote, participate in your neighbourhood association, and work for causes you believe in, they too will believe that ordinary people have the power to change the world.

For better or for worse, we are the living example our children measure the world by and that happens at such a deep, cellular level that we are not usually even aware of it. Our families are where we learn the script for our life roles.

For Example: If you're a woman, think about where your concept of "husband/father" comes from. If your father fixed the plumbing and replaced windows and built a new sundeck, you grow up thinking that this kind of handyman behaviour is what a husband and father do. So when you marry and your husband is useless with a hammer you will probably think he doesn't measure up. But he has his own script of what a wife is supposed to do and chances are you're missing some of the "wife" cues too!

These scripts also pass on the darker side of human behaviour. Someone who observes adults treating each other abusively will think this behaviour is normal. Someone who's grown up using survival techniques like manipulation and lying will continue to use these techniques and expect the same behaviour from their partner. Whether we are aware of it or not, we are passing on the "script" to our kids.

VALUES

Values are absorbed, they're not taught. Live yours and your teen will know where you stand. Live one way and talk another way and you'll have no influence whatsoever.

For Example: Dorea is determined that her daughters will grow up strong and healthy. She lectures them constantly about eating right and taking vitamins. She cooks them big, healthy meals and packs their lunches with cheese and fruit and carrot sticks. But they drive her to distraction, those girls do, because they never eat anything and the school nurse has already warned her that the girls are both borderline anorexic. She's at her wit's end. All the wasted food. That really gets to her. Of course she can't eat it, she's on a diet, always has been, all her life. She lives on grapefruit and cigarettes. There's no way she's getting fat!

Nothing Dorea says will change how her daughters feel about their bodies. She's already been very effective in transferring her values to them.

Sometimes though, it seems as if our values haven't been passed on to our teens. In those cases, it's wise to be patient. Teens often try on different values the same way they try on clothes. They'll try an attitude on

> *Somewhere along the way we realize that we don't know what's best for them anymore. They do.*

just for its shock value and abandon it quickly if they don't have to defend it too vigorously.

"Face" is very important to teens. If they are backed too deeply into a corner by having to defend their beliefs to their parents, and the only way out is to admit they're wrong, they may not be able to do it. It becomes impossible for them to do what their parents want, even if it's what they now want too.

If parents can stay low-key and non-judgmental, they usually find that their values have been absorbed and become those of the teen as well.

Stay approachable when difficult subjects come up. You may never get another chance. If talking about something embarrasses you, say so. But by your example, show that embarrassment is no reason for avoiding difficult subjects.

Don't purposefully avoid conflict. It is an opportunity to teach teens how to resolve conflict. If your own conflict resolution skills are shaky take a conflict resolution course. Parenting teens is a growth experience for parents too and the perfect opportunity to learn some new skills.

If you make a mistake (and you will), simply say so. There's a big difference between giving in because your teen has worn you down and reversing your decision because you've decided your position was wrong. Your teen will know the difference and respect you for admitting a mistake.

Your New Role as Consultant

Remember, most of all, that your role is now evolving from teacher into that of an influential consultant. Although you can and should insist on a code of behaviour consistent with your values in the family home, once your teens walk out that door, they will behave as *they* decide. You cannot force your teen to believe the same things you do, but you can be assured that their own values will have been significantly influenced by everything you do. That's both reassuring and sobering.

~ Chapter Three~

COMMUNICATION

Much More Than Words

As someone brilliant once said, "You can listen your way to a better relationship with your teen, but you'll never talk your way there." So often we have the best of intentions and we just want to help, but some of the things we say throw up walls between us and our teens. This parent-talk doesn't respect the teen's ability to solve their own problems, an ability that needs nurturing, not diminishing. Think about the real message behind some of this well-worn parent-talk:

"What you should do is ..."
"Why don't you ..."
"How come you haven't ..."
"It's not as bad as all that ..."
"It's not as bad as it looks ..."
"Trust me, everything will be fine ..."
"Let's not worry about that now ..."
"What did you do to make her ..."
"You're just too sensitive ..."
"If that's the worst thing that ever happens to you ..."
"The answer is really very simple ..."

Ouch! However well-intentioned, these phrases are put-downs and as far as communication is concerned, shut-downs. Swallow your tongue before you ever let one of these phrases out of your mouth again, because

God gave us two ears, but only one mouth –
there must have been a reason.

these comments have an afterlife. They identify us as someone who does-n't respect others enough to really listen and once we take on that repu-tation it's really, really hard to get anyone (never mind a vulnerable teen) to start confiding in us again.

We need our teens talking to us because adolescence is the bridge between childhood, when parents make the important decisions, and adulthood, when our kids will make decisions for themselves. Learning to make good decisions is the task of adolescence; facilitating that learn-ing is the job of parents.

Parents need to make the transition from instructor (who talks a lot) to guide (who mostly listens). It's not a transition that comes easily or naturally to most of us! But it is a skill we all can learn.

EFFECTIVE LISTENING

Effective listening is probably the most important tool a parent can use to help their teen acquire good decision-making skills. How so? Well, if our teen knows that everything he tells us will be followed by a ten-minute lecture, he will quit telling us what is on his mind. But if he knows that we'll listen attentively, then help him sort through all his options, always respecting him enough to leave the actual decision making up to him, then he'll see us as a resource. He'll want to tell us what's going on in his life.

Effective listening has three components:
> **Listening Attentively**
> **Acknowledging and Reflecting Feelings**
> **Exploring Options and Consequences**

Listening Attentively

When your teen talks to you, listen with your full attention. Put down your paper, turn off the television, turn down the stereo. If the phone rings, let the answering machine get it. Let your teen know, by your actions, that he has your full attention and that he is the most important item on your agenda.

Listen with your eyes as well as your ears. Is your teen uncomfortable with what she's telling you? Is she relaxed, nervous, excited, distressed, or happy? What do her body language, tone of voice, and manner tell you?

Stay focused. How often, when we say we're listening, are we really spending the time marshalling our arguments, building our case, and mentally arranging our points of debate? This isn't a debate. We're not here to make our case. We're here to listen, period.

We need to keep our own responses to a minimum. Our role is to listen, but we should let our teen know that we're hearing them by using phrases such as, "I see," "Uh huh," and so on.

> *If our teen knows that everything he tells us will be followed by a ten-minute lecture, he will quit telling us what is on his mind.*

Acknowledging and Reflecting Their Feelings

Look and listen for the feelings being expressed. They tell us a lot about what is influencing our teen. Feelings are the clues to "why".

Teens often are either unaware of their feelings or just don't seem to have the vocabulary necessary to accurately express what they're feeling. For example, we often say we're "mad". But what we are really feeling is frustrated, humiliated, anxious, angry, scared, insecure, disrespected, or hurt.

Parents perform a valuable role when they can identify teens' feelings with the right words and connect those feelings to the content of issues. Reflecting that information back to teens helps clarify issues for them and shows them that we really do understand.

> *For Example: "It sounds to me like you felt very disrespected when Marie wouldn't take your call."*

If you don't get it right, don't worry, you've opened dialogue about it and you can try again together.

> *For Example: "So it was more a sense of betrayal that you felt then, knowing that some of your other friends were with Marie when you called her?"*

Exploring Options and Consequences

Teaching teens effective problem-solving skills means encouraging them to brainstorm options, then exploring the consequences of these. It's best if the teen comes up with these options themselves, but some prompting may be necessary. Use encouraging questions like:

> *"What do you think you might do?"*
> *"What else could you try?"*
> *"How have you seen your friends handle this?"*
> *"What other ideas might work?"*

Do not put down any of these ideas or offer your opinion about any of them. If asked, simply say, "It's an option."

After brainstorming options, guide your teen into exploring the consequences of each option. If possible, keep your comments to yourself. If specifically asked what you think, go ahead and offer your thoughts, but try to keep the focus on the teen figuring this stuff out for herself. Use questions like:

> *"What do you think would happen if you did that?"*
> *"Do you think that would improve the situation?"*
> *"What has happened when other people tried that?"*
> *"Is that result something you could live with?"*

You won't always be there to make your teen's choices for her, so stayed focused on your job here – to help her learn how to make decisions. It's important that your teen takes responsibility for deciding which option to take. It's very, very difficult for a parent to watch their teen walk straight into the face of a mistake, but mistakes are how we learn *not* to do something. Let your teen make mistakes in less-than-life-threatening situations.

EFFECTIVE TALKING

How much of what we call 'talking' is really 'talking at". Disguised as "talking" many of the following sneak into our homes: nagging, criticizing, cajoling, threatening, lecturing, questioning, advising, evaluating, probing, ridiculing, grilling, and so on. These tactics destroy rather than improve any hope of communicating with our teen.

Another technique that shuts down communication is what the experts call "Closed Responses." Here's an example:

Closed Response

> *Daughter: "I'm really pissed off at Joel for not showing up tonight."*
> *Father: "Well that's about what you'd expect from a guy like him isn't it? Might as well get used to it. That's life, Babe."*

Open Response

> *Daughter: "I'm really pissed off at Joel for not showing up tonight."*
> *Father: "Yeah, I can see that you're upset about it."*

It's fairly obvious why the "Closed Response" is a put-down that will either cause the teen to clam up and go watch MTV or get into a fight defending Joel to her father. In the second example the daughter is encouraged to continue talking because her father has demonstrated that he's really heard and understood how she feels.

I MESSAGES

Another technique, now so well-promoted that you may already be using it, is called the *I MESSAGE*. It is a very effective way of talking to teens, because it shifts the emphasis off blaming the teen (which encourages argument) to how the parent feels about the teen's behaviour. *I MESSAGES* are non-threatening, which means the teen is more likely to hear what the parent is saying. They also give the teen very clear information about what the parent expects.

I MESSAGES work best in a firm, but calm tone of voice so, if you're very angry, give yourself time to cool off before re-approaching your teen.

How to Deliver an I MESSAGE

1. Name the behaviour or situation you want changed.
   Aim this statement at the behaviour, not the teen or their personality. Start with "When I..."
   For Example: "When I find your hockey gear lying all over the living room ..."

2. Say how you feel about the situation.
   We often believe the emotion that we are feeling is anger, but if we look a little closer we realize that it is actually fear, hurt, disrespect, or worry. Think out your statement ahead of time and try to use an accurately descriptive word. Start with "I feel ..."
   For Example: "I feel disgusted ..."

3. State your reason or the consequence to you.
   Everyone needs a reason to change their behaviour. Give your teen the real reason and begin with "because ..."
   For Example: " ...because it smells horrible and when I first get up in the morning it really nauseates me."

4. Say what you want done.
   Be explicit. Start with "I would like ..."
   For Example: "I would like you to put your hockey gear in the garage to dry out and keep it out of the house."

Complete I MESSAGE
   "When I find your hockey gear lying all over the living room. I feel disgusted because it smells horrible and it really nauseates me. I would like you to put your hockey gear in the garage to dry out and keep it out of the house."

Ask for Agreement
   Follow your *I MESSAGE* with a request for agreement and commitment.
   For Example: "Will you dry your hockey gear out in the garage and keep it out of the house?"

*Even their brains are under reconstruction, increasing
in size by at least one-third.*

ARGUING

Parenting a child between ages eight and eleven is usually a pleasant experience. In the continuum of life, ages eight to eleven or so, are pretty peaceful. It's very easy for a parent to get smug and think that they've got this parenting gig under control. At this age, kids tend to adore their parents and think they know everything. Ah, it is a blissful time.

Blissful but short lived, because overnight, hormones start pulsing through their system, creating a whole new personality. It might even feel like a stranger has moved into their room. Their emotions may short circuit, sparking from one extreme to another, while their bodies lurch out of control into adult form. Even their brains are under reconstruction, increasing in size by at least one-third. A child's brain is equipped to deal with what is. The adolescent brain is now able to contemplate what might be.

What this means to parental peace is – the end. Teens eagerly exercise their newly discovered intellectual capacity and, since they've recently discovered that they now know more than you do about pretty much everything, it's easy to get sucked into arguing with them. Like a toddler who has just learned to walk and must run everywhere – just for the joy of it – a teen argues.

If a parent can keep that perspective – that arguing is a stage in their teen's intellectual development just like body hair is a stage in their physical development – it is much easier to deal with. Just as a toddler will get over the newness of walking, a teen will grow accustomed to their expanded intellectual capacity and turn their attention elsewhere.

Remember though, that teens aren't delivered out of cookie cutters. One teen may drive his parent to absolute distraction arguing about everything, while his sibling skips right over this phase of intellectual development. And while one teen will hit his intellectual stride at thirteen, another will wait till she's eighteen to spring start arguing with them, just when they thought they were in the clear. There are no absolutes about adolescence.

A teen's unrelenting push for independence runs smack up against our foot on the brake. And when they throw some attitude into it, there's no way this isn't going to lead to conflict.

ANGER

I don't think anyone is as capable of routinely, day-in-and-day-out making us as angry as a teen. There are a number of reasons for this. A teen's unrelenting push for independence runs smack up against our foot on the brake. And when they throw some attitude into it, there's no way this isn't going to lead to conflict. It reminds me of when my oldest son was about four years old. While walking down a busy street one day he suddenly wrenched his hand out of mine and darted towards the traffic. My reflexes were good and I managed to grab him back, but the emotions that pumped through me were a schizophrenic mix of anger and terror. I was physically sick at the vision of what might have happened to my little boy under the wheels of an oncoming vehicle, but at the same time I was so angry with him that I felt like I could have killed him on the spot myself.

Not dissimilar are my fears for my teens. I read the newspaper. I watch

I'm a mother. My nightmares play out in living colour.

the news. I know, in great detail, how truly dangerous the world can be. I'm a mother. My nightmares play out in living colour. Intellectually I know that I can't hold my teen's hand forever, but that loosening has to happen at a pace that even if I'm not exactly comfortable with, doesn't leave me terror stricken either.

When my fears for them are treated as ridiculous and they regard me as if I were some kind of simpleton living in another century, it makes me angry. When their eyes roll, or they mutter dismissive messages under their breath (but loud enough for me to almost hear), or they use gestures, mannerisms, or words specifically designed to make me lose my cool, I get angry.

Your teen has been living with you for many years. They know where all your buttons are. They are naturally self-centred at this age and when they want something badly enough they'll push every one and you will get angry.

The most helpful piece of advice I have ever been given was to refuse to make decisions when I am angry. Very often we are angry in the first place because our teen has pushed and pushed and pushed us. They want something and they figure that if they just keep hammering at us they will exhaust us and we'll get so anxious to get them out of our face that we'll say "Yes". They'll get what they want. Don't let this scenario become the modus operandi in your house because it's a miserable way to operate. If hammering away at you gets them the results they want, they will never give up. They're younger than us, their stamina is better and they're motivated!

When you're being hammered at tell them you are too angry, exhausted, or confused to think right at the moment and that you'll need more time. If they continue to push, tell them that if they keep it up you are most likely to make the decision they don't want to hear, "No". Explain that it is definitely in their best interest to leave you alone until you've calmed down. Try to give them a definite time for when you will

Human beings haven't figured out how to make time yet and in our busy lives today we will never find it. Take it.

have a decision for them, say 3:00, or tomorrow morning, or the end of the month! Then physically remove yourself from the situation. Lock the bathroom door and get into the shower, go for a walk, or get in the car and drive away if you have to. If, for some reason, they are able to pursue you, then make good on your promise to give them the decision they don't want, "No". And stick to it.

Just accepting that conflict is the logical spinoff when an adolescent's quest for freedom runs up against a parent's instinct to stomp on the brake, will help you keep the parent/teen relationship in perspective and your anger under control. Conflict, and the emotion it generates – anger, is normal.

While the hammering tactics must be minimized if you're going to survive to collect your pension, conflict itself should not be avoided. Just the opposite. For better or for worse, a parent is their teen's role model and conflict is an opportunity to model communication and conflict resolution skills. Some good information about conflict resolution techniques are set out in *Chapter Ten*. Your "parenting-teen-years" are the perfect time to brush up your conflict resolution skills (told you this parenting teens stuff was going to be a growth experience). Take a conflict resolution course through your local community centre or continuing education department. Better yet, look for a course that welcomes both parents and teens.

You should also be aware that conflict with teens often triggers unresolved issues from our own teenage years, which may interfere with our ability to communicate with our teens. As parents we need to review our own teen years and settle any outstanding issues we might still have, particularly with our own parents. Your teen knows where all your sensitive buttons are and sooner or later she'll push every one. Diffuse the dynamite that's hiding behind them.

ENCOURAGING COMMUNICATION

How you feel about your teen is irrelevant. What matters is what they think you feel about them. Listen for clues about this, then look for opportunities to communicate your belief in them.

Take Time

Take one-on-one time for you and your teen on a regular, scheduled basis. If you wait until you can find the time or think that sometime soon you'll make the time, you won't. Human beings haven't figured out how to make time yet and in our busy lives today we will never find it. *Take it.*

Why schedule time instead of just enjoying spontaneous moments? Well, it's not a case of "instead of". Continue to grab those spontaneous moments of fun and closeness but don't depend on them to do the job of building a close relationship with your teen. Spontaneity is too dependent on our being available and alert and ready to rock at a moment's notice. Those kinds of moments just don't happen often enough.

It's like saving for retirement. If we wait until we have some spare cash to invest in mutual funds we'll never do it. Smart people get the bank or their payroll department to make automatic withdrawals each month. It's the only reliable way to build equity.

So it is with your kids. Together, look for opportunities to do things that you would both genuinely enjoy doing with each other: take in a movie on $2 Tuesdays; play tennis on Saturday mornings; refinish a piece of furniture together; walk on Sunday evenings; take guitar lessons; rebuild an engine.

The important ingredients are:
- *scheduling the time together on a regular basis;*
- *choosing an activity you both enjoy; and*
- *ensuring the time is for fun only.*

The last ingredient, "fun only", is very important. There are other times to give "I Messages" about the mess in the kitchen or to teach important life lessons. These one-on-one times are for enjoying each other's company, period. The equity these times build is invaluable. And furthermore, teens are fun. Enjoy each other and communication will come naturally.

Respect Them

On that bridge between childhood and adult life, teens are particularly sensitive about not being treated as children. How we talk to them can be flashpoints of irritation for them, meaning that whatever we're trying to communicate to them is lost while they're busy being angry about being talked to as if they were children.

The easiest way to retrain yourself into talking to them as the adults they're straining to become, is to simply do that. Imagine you're talking to a friend or colleague. This will neutralize your language and make it easier for the message you're trying to deliver to be heard.

Stay Approachable

Stay approachable when difficult subjects come up. You may never get another chance. If talking about something embarrasses you, say so. By your example, show them that embarrassment is not a reason for avoiding difficult subjects. Just be honest.

Parents frequently report that the car often offers irreplaceable opportunities for both raising difficult topics and getting to know their teen better. It's easy to get impatient with how often we're needed to fetch and deliver a carload of giggling and guffawing teens. But I think chauffeur duties give a parent the most incredible insight into their teen's world. I think of it in terms of those windows that National Geographic cameramen build into animal dens so they can film animals having sex and giving birth. I don't think any of my kid's friends have had sex in the back seat of my car while I was driving down the freeway, but I have heard some really interesting stuff. Since they're in my car and I'm not using any technological assistance to hear these conversations I don't believe it is eavesdropping, but I don't think it would be a good idea to admit that I'd heard this stuff. So I just treat this information as what journalists call "deep background" – unusable and unsourcable, but providing much insight!

The car is also the place where a great many sensitive conversations happen when it's just parent and teen. Sitting side by side, the teen doesn't have to look directly into your face and may feel more free to bring up things or respond to your inquiries.

Use neutral, impersonal situations to approach difficult subjects:

*I don't think any of my kid's friends have had sex in the back
seat of my car while I was driving down the freeway, but I
have heard some really interesting stuff.*

Ask them what they think about a particular ad campaign about AIDS.

"Do you think that billboard is going to change how people behave?"

Comment on a celebrity's appearance.

*"When I see how thin that model looks in those ads I can't help won-
dering if she'll ever be able to have children."*

Ask them what they think about a celebrity's divorce or drug charges
or public behaviour.

*"I wonder what makes someone like that actor lose control of his life
like that?"* or *"That singer always looks so sad in her pictures, do
you think she's suicidal?"*

Conversation starters like these can open the way to a more personal
discussion, either about something you want to bring up with them or
something you think they may want to talk to you about. If they just
grunt and don't appear to want to talk about it, let it drop. You've delivered the message that you're willing to talk about these subjects. When

they're ready, they'll return to the subject. When that happens, be sensitive to it. Their opener may be quite subtle. You may not get another chance.

Communication is Much More Than Words

As parents we sometimes feel that we're not getting through to our teens. On a verbal level, this may well be true. Teens don't learn much from being talked at. Remember though, that we communicate with everything we do.

- *If we put down our paper and give a teen our full attention when they speak to us, we're saying that we care enough about them to give them our full attention.*
- *When we cancel our golf game so we can be at their hockey tournament, we're telling them that they are the most important.*
- *When we spend the night at the movies with them, we're saying that we enjoy their company.*
- *When we ask our teen to help us choose a new computer for the office, we're saying that we respect their expertise.*
- *When we use respectful language toward them, even when we're very angry, we're making it clear that this is the standard in our household.*
- *When we treat everyone we meet with respect, we're teaching that all people are equal.*
- *When we vote, volunteer in the community and work for causes we believe in we're demonstrating our faith that ordinary people change the world.*

Being aware of the many levels on which we communicate can be both reassuring and cause for concern: concern, if we don't like the messages we've been sending; but reassurance when we understand that even though it may seem like our verbal messages are being ignored, the non-verbal messages will be absorbed.

~ Chapter Four ~

VALUES

...you're wearing yours!

This chapter is about what we commonly call "values". We all have them. Values are simply the worth each of us puts on issues like monogamous sexuality, education, money, honesty, drug use, democracy, marriage, sobriety, religious affiliation, and so on. These can be controversial issues. They are also one of the most critical heritages we pass on to our children and parents are often very concerned about doing this effectively.

If you haven't actually taken the time to think through how you feel about issues you may not even be consciously aware of what your values are. Be aware however, we wear our values quite publicly.

For Example:
- *If we always drink when we party, we are saying that we can't have a good time without alcohol.*
- *If we smuggle goods through the border, we are telling our kids that it's okay to lie.*
- *If we know that our friend is beating his wife but never confront him, we're saying that spousal abuse is okay.*
- *If when our son has trouble in school we start taking our lunch to work instead of buying it, so that we can afford a tutor for him, we are saying that education (and he) is very important.*
- *If we attend church and regularly give a portion of the family income to support that faith, we are communicating that we value our religious faith.*

We wear our values publicly.

- *If we are faithful to our spouse and regularly make time to be alone with him or her, we are showing that we value marriage.*
- *If we vote in every election and volunteer for activist causes, we are communicating our belief that as individuals we are not helpless. We can change the world.*

Values are not something we decide one day to start teaching our adolescent children. We've been communicating our values to our children throughout their whole lives. We should, however, be prepared to have our values challenged. Teens are very big on that.

Define Your Values

Defining one's own values means sitting down and really thinking through what we believe about the issues that are likely to come up with our teen.

> *For Example: Ask yourself, "What are my beliefs about sex?"*
> * *Anytime, anywhere, at any age?*
> * *Only within marriage?*
> * *Okay in a committed relationship after age eighteen?*
> * *As long as it's not in my house and I don't know about it?*

Think about this issue, and all the other "value" issues like: alcohol and other drugs, pornography, money, religious affiliation, monogamy, honesty, and so on. If you have a partner, discuss these issues with him or her. You don't have to agree, but in many cases you will need to present a common front on what is acceptable in your household. Coming home one evening to find a dozen drunk teenagers in your basement is not the time to discover that one of you thinks this is funny while the other one is ready to call in the militia and hang the bootlegger.

You are the Model

Think about what you did as a teenager and how you're going to marry that up with what you want for your kids. If you and your siblings sit around at family gatherings regaling each other with stories about all the nights you climbed in the basement window so drunk that you don't even remember driving home, you won't have much luck convincing your teens they shouldn't drink and drive.

If this kind of glorification of the illegal, unsafe and/or destructive behaviours of your youth has been part of the entertainment when you get together with old friends or family, talk to them about how these stories will affect any kids who are listening. And don't think that just because they're in bed they're out of earshot. Kids love hearing how "bad" Mom or Dad was, and they'll have no scruples about creeping down the hall to eavesdrop on the war stories. Once people understand how much interest kids take in these stories, and that by glorifying these activities (and the stories do get bigger and better with time) they're modelling behaviours like "drinking is nothing but fun, fun, fun" they should be willing to stop. If they don't care enough about your kids to do this, seriously reconsider having these people in your home and around your kids.

We are our children's models – it's that simple. If we have done things in our own past that we hope they don't do, and they ask about them, the truth is usually best. For instance, you could say:

"As a teen I did smoke some dope, but I know a lot more about it now and I wouldn't make the same decision today because..."

Don't get taken by surprise. Kids will ask these questions. Think through your values. Discuss them with your partner. Be ready with your answer. Know what you want for your teens and why.

Parents as Consultants

Realize that in the area of values we are consultants. We can, and should, be firm about what happens under our own roof, but the truth is, that once those kids walk out the door they will make the choices that they think are best for themselves. Thinking we have any control outside our own home is an illusion – influence, yes, but control, no.

Teens Go For Shock Value

Teens like to try on values the way they try on "looks". Sometimes they'll try something (like green hair) on and wear it around for a week or two just for the shock value. Kids love to perform and arguing with parents is a major source of entertainment.

For Example: A teen whose mother is active with a political party could declare he supported the opposing party and to prove it, hang party placards out his bedroom window. This could be embarrassing for his parents and they could get in a huge power struggle with him over this, but it would be such a waste of time and energy.

First of all, arguing would merely entrench his position and if he were forced to invest too much of himself in this position it could make it impossible for him to abandon it. We need to be careful that we don't make our teens defend themselves so vigorously that they would lose face if they wanted to backtrack. Don't make it impossible for your teen to agree with you.

Secondly, politics are an issue over which a teen's parents have absolutely no control. When he is old enough to vote he will go into the

We need to be careful that we don't make our teens defend themselves so vigorously that they would lose face if they wanted to backtrack.

polling station by himself and vote for whomever his own personal values tell him to vote for. After a lifetime of living with parents who've supported a particular political ideology, he will probably be influenced to vote as they do, but this is an issue of influence, not control.

Don't Wait Till It's Personal

Don't wait for a major blow-up with your teen to talk about values issues. For example, not discussing your expectations around alcohol use until your teen comes home drunk is not a great idea. At that time you'll both be upset and emotional and, in his or her case, either drunk or hungover. The issue will have become personal and the teen will feel that they have to defend both their behaviour and the alcohol industry in general!

Instead, look for opportunities to talk about these issues before they become personal. Use celebrities in the news, movies you're both watching and commercials you see on television to open the conversation and help you explore your teen's attitudes and opinions. You may be surprised. One mother reported that she'd assumed she'd have to make rules and "get tough" about alcohol use, but once she talked to her kids she was surprised by their attitudes. They told her that they thought drinking was "dumb". You see, she'd always been a non-drinker and modelled that alcohol didn't have anything to do with having a good time. On the other hand, her kids had watched their uncles drinking at family gatherings. Having observed their uncles' behaviour disintegrate from happy and full of fun early on, to belligerent and argumentative as their drinking continued through the evening, the kids had come to their own conclusion that drinking is "dumb".

When you're talking to your teen about values, be particularly respectful of their opinions. Avoid communication blocks, especially put

Educate yourself and appeal to their reason, don't try to impose your will through authority.

downs that infer that "at their age they're in no position to make important decisions that will affect the rest of their lives". The fact is, that every day they are making decisions that will affect the rest of their lives and as parents we'll have the most influence with them if we respect that. Ask questions and carefully listen for the answers. You may be surprised at the wisdom your kids show. Listen for their thoughts and feelings and approach from a position of respect, not judgment. Educate yourself and appeal to their reason, don't try to impose your will through authority. When it comes to developing a system of values, each person does it for him or herself. "Authority" carries no weight here.

PEER PRESSURE ...It's Mostly Good

Many people assume that "peer pressure" is bad. This assumption is really disrespectful of teens because much, if not most, peer pressure is positive. Teens bolster each other's self esteem, prop each other up, commiserate with each other, encourage each other, and help each other with their problems both in terms of psychological support and concrete assistance with things like homework, clothes, getting jobs, helping with chores, and loaning money. They are each other's best friends and at no time in life is that network more supportive and important than during adolescence. They give each other the sense of belonging that is so important to teens' emotional well-being.

Don't be too quick to judge either. The teens we, as parents, are most likely to think would be a good influence on our son or daughter, may not be. They may just be really good at conning adults. The kid who looks like a rebel may be the one with the kind of backbone to help our kid get out of a sticky situation sometime. After all, it takes guts to stand out in a crowd.

Respect their ability to make good choices about their friends; they have a lot more insider information than you do. One father recounted

Respect their ability to make good choices
about their friends; they have a lot more
insider information than you do.

how his son finally blew up at him one day, saying "Dad, you keep push-ing me to spend time with Jordan just because you know his parents and you think he's a good kid but you don't know anything, Dad. Jordan is the biggest pusher in the school."

When Peer Pressure Isn't Positive

A constructive way to approach negative peer pressure is from the angle that you believe they know what is best for themselves. Promote the concept that only wimps and wusses let other people make their decisions for them. They, on the other hand, are smart and capable and the ones who should be in charge of deciding what is best for themselves. You'll find strategies for teaching them how to say "no" and mean it in the *Chapter Ten*.

The most important factor in resisting peer pressure is a teen's strong sense of his or her own worth and value. The more confident and capa-ble teens feel and the more experience they have with decision making for themselves, the "safer" they will be.

The secret to making kids resistant to negative peer pressure? Value them, so that they value themselves and believe in their own ability and right to make the best decisions for themselves.

INSTILLING VALUES ~ ASSET BUILDING

I've often wished there were a vaccine that would protect our kids from alcohol and drug abuse, from engaging in sexual activity or violent behaviour, or from depression and suicide. I wished there were a magic potion that would promote positive attitudes and make kids want to suc-ceed in school and look after themselves.

Now the Search Institute of Minneapolis, Minnesota has identified the forty developmental assets that, if they don't actually vaccinate kids against harm, go a long way towards tipping the odds in their favour. The

40 Developmental Assets

EXTERNAL ASSETS

Support

- ❏ Family support - Family life provides high levels of love and support.
- ❏ Positive family communication - Parents and youth communicate positively - youth is willing to seek parents advice and counsel.
- ❏ Other adult relationships - youth receives support from three or more non-parent adults.
- ❏ Caring neighbourhood - Youth experiences caring neighbours.
- ❏ Caring school climate - School provides a caring, encouraging environment.
- ❏ Parent involvement in schooling - Parents are actively involved in helping youth succeed in school.

Empowerment

- ❏ Community values youth - Youth perceives that community adults value youth.
- ❏ Youth given useful roles - Youth are given useful roles in community life.
- ❏ Community service - Youth gives one hour or more per week to serving in one's community.
- ❏ Safety - Youth feels safe in home, school and neighbourhood.

Boundaries And Expectations

- ❏ Family boundaries - Family has clear rules and consequences; and monitors whereabouts.
- ❏ School boundaries - School provides clear rules and consequences.
- ❏ Neighbourhood boundaries - Neighbours would report undesirable behaviour to family.
- ❏ Adult role models - Parent(s) and other adults model prosocial behaviour.
- ❏ Positive peer influence - Youth's best friends model responsible behaviour.
- ❏ High Expectations - Both parents and teachers press youth to achieve.

Time Use

- ❏ Creative activities - Involved in three or more hours per week in lessons or practice in music, theatre, or other arts.
- ❏ Youth programs - Involved three hours or more per week in sports, clubs, or organizations at school and/or in community organizations.
- ❏ Religious community - Involved one or more hours per week.
- ❏ Time at home - Out with friends "with nothing special to do," two or fewer nights per week.

INTERNAL ASSETS

Educational Commitment

❏ Achievement motivation - Youth is motivated to do well in school.

❏ School engagement - Youth is actively engaged in school.

❏ Homework - Youth reports one or more hours of homework per day.

❏ Bonding to school - Youth cares about her/his school.

❏ Reading for pleasure - Youth reads for pleasure three or more hours per week.

Values

❏ Caring - Youth places high value on helping other people.

❏ Equality and social justice - Youth places high value on promoting equality and reducing hunger and poverty.

❏ Integrity - Youth acts on convictions, stands up for her or his beliefs.

❏ Honesty - Youth "tells the truth even when it is not easy".

❏ Responsibility - Youth accepts and takes personal responsibility.

❏ Restraint - Youth believes it is important not to be sexually active or to use alcohol or other drugs.

Social Competencies

❏ Planning and decision making - Youth has skill to plan ahead and make choices.

❏ Interpersonal competence - Youth has empathy, sensitivity and friendship skills.

❏ Cultural competence - Youth has knowledge of and comfort with people of different racial backgrounds.

❏ Resistance skills - Youth can resist negative peer pressure.

❏ Nonviolent conflict resolution - Youth seeks to resolve conflict non- violently.

Positive Identity

❏ Personal control - Youth feels she/he has control over "things that happen to me".

❏ Self-esteem - Youth reports high self-esteem.

❏ Sense of purpose - Youth reports "my life has a purpose".

❏ Positive view of personal future - Youth is optimistic about his/her personal future.

This list of forty developmental assets has been reprinted with the permission of the Search Institute of Minneapolis, MN. If you would like more information about Asset Building, please visit the Search Institute's website at **www.search-institute.org** or call them at (612)376-8955, toll free 1-800-888-7828, or write Search Institute, 700 Third Street, Suite 210, Minneapolis, MN, 55415.

beauty of this concept is that every person who cares about kids can look at the list of developmental assets and pick off a couple to work at each day with the kids within their realm of influence. Whether it is as a parent, grandparent, teacher, coach, employer, or neighbour, we all have a role to play in the lives of all the kids around us.

Asset Building isn't a program that parents enrol in or a course that we sign up for – it's a case of plugging this new information about what grows healthy kids into our current parenting practices. Thoughtful, caring parents instinctively encourage these assets in their kids anyway. However, by doing the solid, credible research that documents what we instinctively know, the Search Institute has provided us all with a specific list of assets and the proof that investing in developing these assets pays off.

For example, when teens have:
- *21 to 40 of these assets, only 14% engage in problem alcohol use, 6% in illicit drug use, and 10% in sexual activity.*
- *31 to 40 assets, the percentage with alcohol problems drops to 3%, illicit drug use to 1%, and sexual activity drops to 3%.*

Developing these assets also promotes positive behaviours.

For example, of teens with 31 to 40 assets,
- *53% are very successful in school,*
- *88% maintain good health, and*
- *72% willingly delay gratification.*

It's obvious that proactively developing these assets in our kids has positive results for their health and well-being. Thanks to the Search Institute we all have a definitive list of assets with which to work.

As a parent, review the list of assets, identifying those you believe each of your teens has developed. Then work through the list with your teen, asking them which assets they believe they have. By comparing your two lists, the parent and teen will have a personalized inventory of assets that need further development.

~ Chapter Five ~

ABOUT SEX

A teenage boy I met phrased it particularly well. He said, "Parents always say that they are willing to talk about sex, but that's just not true. What they want to talk about is *not* having sex."

Even for adults, talking about *how* to talk to teens about sex is a bit of a sticky wicket. Some parents assume their teens will "do it" and are all for stuffing their pockets with condoms. Other parents believe that if they scream, "No! No! No!" loud enough and often enough, their kids just won't do it.

My position is that while we as parents may have some influence, a teen will make his or her own decision based on their own, internally evolved value system. Whatever I, as a parent may wish, hope, and pray my children do is one thing; my *job* as a parent is to make sure they are prepared. These days, sex can be fatal. Don't leave your teen's education to a magazine or a rock star or daytime television. Make sure your teens know everything they need to know, both to make the best decision for themselves and to keep themselves safe when they decide to have sex. Think about it. Sooner or later, inside or outside of marriage, your son or daughter will have sex. They need accurate information and it's your job to give it.

If you are embarrassed, say so. Let them know that embarrassment is no excuse for avoiding difficult subjects. They'll appreciate that.

We value them when we honour
the decisions that they make for
themselves, even when they differ
from what we'd do.

Their Reasons

Some of the top reasons teens give for having sex are:
- to hold onto a boyfriend or girlfriend
- to feel grownup
- to feel loved

A teen who has grown up feeling valued, values him or herself. They are not as vulnerable to the need to "hold onto" someone for their identity and they already feel loved. They know they are not "grown up" and are willing to wait for that to happen.

The most important thing you can do to influence your teen's decision about when and with whom to have sex, is to simply let them know how much you value them. "Self" esteem really isn't a self-generated thing. How we feel about ourselves is much more a reflected kind of thing. When other people value us and let us know that, we feel good about ourselves. It would be difficult to keep having faith in ourselves if all that was ever reflected back at us was how unworthy we were. The most important people in a teen's life are his or her parents. It stands to reason then, that our opinion of them would be most influential in how valued they feel.

How do we show value? By listening respectfully to them, by genuinely taking their opinions into account when making parental decisions, and by asking their advice in their areas of expertise, then following that advice. We value them when we honour the decisions that they make for themselves, even when they differ from what we'd do. We demonstrate that we value them when we make time for them one-on-one and when we express, often and wholeheartedly, how glad we are that they are our son or daughter.

CLARIFY YOUR OWN VALUES

Before we can hope to influence our teens, we need to be certain of our own beliefs. Think about the following issues (and others that come to mind). If you have a partner, talk them over together. You don't necessarily have to agree on everything, but discuss your differences in private before the issue comes up with your teen:

- *What is the purpose of sexuality? Is it to have babies, to have fun, or to share love?*
- *What about recreational sex? Do you have to love someone and be married to them, or willing to marry them? Is liking them enough?*
- *How old is old enough for sex?*
- *Are you willing to have people who aren't married sleep together in your home?*
- *If so, can your son or daughter have their boyfriend or girlfriend sleep over in their room?*
- *How do you feel about fidelity?*
- *How do you feel about homosexuality?*
- *What about birth control? Abortion?*
- *Are you comfortable with your son or daughter masturbating? If so, are you comfortable enough to recommend it as a way to work off sexual steam?*

As you can see, there is a great deal to think about. Don't avoid it, because you will be challenged. Teens love to push limits, so you'd better know where yours are.

Modelling Healthy Sexual Values

Our major areas of influence with teens are in the contributions we've made to their sense of self-worth and in the example we model in our own lives. For many years they've been keenly observing our behaviour and making their own judgments about it. We've no idea how influential that modelling has been.

One young woman, who had any number of serious emotional problems in other areas of her life, told me once that, "Thank goodness, sex is one thing I'm really comfortable with." It seems that her parents, although they fought a lot and weren't too great at communicating over issues, had always been obvious about their lust for each other. The kids all knew that when Mom was in the kitchen alone washing dishes Dad

The kids weren't supposed to see any of the little "grabs and giggles" that went on, but they did and they found it very reassuring.

liked to sneak up behind her and had actually been observed grabbing her breasts. Mom would giggle and chase him away by throwing soap-suds at him. The kids weren't supposed to see any of this, or the other little "grabs and giggles" that went on, but they did and they found it very reassuring. They learned that while Mom and Dad didn't always get along over the chequebook, they really liked each other. This behaviour set up expectations in their children that sex would be an exciting, unifying perk in marriage.

Each generation of teens believes that sex belongs to them, the youthful. The source of that belief is the widely believed "fact" that males achieve their sexual prime at eighteen. Well, it turns out that a male is in his prime at eighteen, but it's his genital prime. This means he's probably capable of shooting off several healthy rounds per hour with no appar-

It turns out that a male is in his prime at eighteen, but it's his "genital" prime.

ent need to reload, and it probably means that he's shooting more live ammunition per fluid ounce than his forty-five-year-old father, but it does not mean that he knows the first thing about making love.

Not only do teens like to think that sex belongs to them, they tend to think, after sitting through a couple sex education classes at school, that they know everything about it. I well remember one conversation I had with a fourteen-year-old who told me that he did, indeed, know everything there was to know. "So," I responded as casually as possible, "You'll know what to do then, when you can't get it up?" His head snapped up and his eyes nearly popped out of their sockets. "That happens?" he screeched. Oh, I am mean, I thought. But it worked. We went on to have a great conversation about the emotional aspects of sexual arousal and how stresses in other areas of our lives can be reflected in our ability to enjoy sex. We also talked about the effects of alcohol and other drugs, the long-term effects of anabolic steroids, and so on. It was amazing, how once that know-it-all facade cracked, he was open and eager to talk about a whole range of values issues.

Be a Consultant

But remember, it's a case of talking about, not preaching at. Just keep reminding yourself that, around values issues, you are now a consultant. Be an "askable" parent, someone kids can come to for straight-goods information. Stick to facts and choke back your natural-born need to moralize!

> *For Example: Jenn's mother overhears her daughter and her friends arguing about the failure rate of the pill. When she comes into the room they ask her, "Mrs. J., we have to do this project for sex ed and we're wondering if you know what the failure rate of the pill is. Kit says its 5% but I think it's only 1%."*
> *Mrs. J. responds, "I can't believe you girls are even discussing this. Do your parents know? I can't imagine what's got into your teacher's heads talking about this nonsense in class. Someday you'll get married and when that happens you can ask the doctor all these questions. Until then ...well, I wouldn't dream of asking my mother questions like these."*

And frankly, those kids wouldn't dream of asking this mother anything about sex ever again either. When they asked Elle's mother, though, they got a different response.

> *"Well, I'm not sure actually. I suspect it's probably closer to 5%, but even at 1%, that's pretty scary, isn't it? I mean, think of how many thousands of times in her lifetime a woman is going to have sex. Even with a failure rate of one out of one hundred, the odds on her getting pregnant are awfully high. If I really didn't want to get pregnant I certainly wouldn't trust just the pill. And the pill doesn't give any protection against sexually transmitted diseases does it?"*

Elle's mother certainly hopes that her daughter and her friends don't have sex for a long time yet, either, but her approach to answering the girls' question makes her an askable parent. It's factual, respectful, tells the girls what she would do, but doesn't preach at them about what they should do. She finishes with a question, inviting the conversation to continue. It seems likely that it would and that the girls' next question would be to ask her what she would do. Her response might be:

> *"Well, between the worry about pregnancy and the fact that now, with AIDS, sex can kill you, I'd have to think really carefully, first of all, about whether or not to have sex with someone. I wouldn't want to be rushed or feel like I was being pushed. If someone was doing that to me, I guess I'd think that he didn't really care about me and that would kind of answer the question for me."*

The conversation is now ongoing and she has become an askable parent. She understands that by staying low-key and non-judgmental she has the opportunity to be very influential.

THE FACTS

Educate yourself. The schools all have sex education classes, practically from kindergarten now, so your kids may well know more than you do about the nuts and bolts of it. Get yourself up to speed. You'll blow your credibility with them if you don't. On the other hand, don't be intimidated by the school system or figure you'll just leave it up to them. You need the facts to make sure you're credible, but as a parent, you put your own spin on the presentation.

A sex education class, for instance, may teach the facts around failure rates for various birth control devices. This makes birth control devices with lower rates look attractive. A parent, however, can point out that even a failure rate of 1% which sounds low, is a pregnancy rate of 1/100 – much too high for a teen who isn't ready to be a parent.

But If I Talk About Birth Control...

Aren't I condoning promiscuous sex just by talking about it? Aren't I giving my teen permission to go out and have sex? I just can't do this.

Listen up:
- sex can be fatal;
- AIDS is spreading rapidly through the teen population;
- sex kills;
- teens are in real danger;
- teens decide for themselves when to have sex;
- it is very unlikely that they will tell you before they do have sex;
- you will have no warning;
- you have no control over whether or not your teen will have sex;
- sooner or later, in or out of marriage, they will have sex.

Get your head out of the sand and make sure you've prepared them.

Don't misunderstand me. Use every bit of influence you have to try and persuade your son or daughter to wait for a long-term, committed, and monogamous relationship before they have sex. Tell them this. Tell them exactly what you hope and pray for them. Then make sure they have all the information they need to be safe. Because they may *choose* to make a different decision.

If you're uncomfortable talking about birth control and sexually transmitted diseases (STDs) because you're concerned that giving your teen this kind of information may be interpreted as condoning it, say so. They're not stupid. Say something like the following:

"As you know, my position on sex is that it should be saved for marriage. We've discussed this already and you know all my reasons for thinking this is the best. But I also understand that you're growing up – you're already well on your way to becoming an adult and you

One book I read suggested giving each teen both a cucumber and a condom so they could practise under the parent's supervision!

will make whatever decisions you think are best for you. Therefore, even though I have reservations about this and even though I am concerned you'll interpret this conversation as a green light to have sex, I want to make sure you have all the facts around birth control and the prevention of sexually transmitted diseases."

Besides, knowing how difficult this conversation is for you, your teen is getting a loud, clear message that you value them greatly. They know that whatever decisions they make in the future, you respect their right to make them and will love them no matter what.

If your teens wait until their first sexual encounter to fumble around trying to get a condom out of the package and on, chances are high they will discard it altogether.

About Condoms

Do condoms keep sexually active people 100% safe from pregnancy and STDs? No, but at the moment they are one of the most important safeguards we have. Make sure your teens, both boys and girls, know how to use one. Remember that sooner or later, inside of marriage or outside of marriage, they will have sex and they need to be prepared.

If your teens wait until their first sexual encounter to fumble around trying to get a condom out of the package and on for the first time, chances are good that they will be so embarrassed by their fumbling that they will either not put it on correctly or they will discard it altogether. One book I read suggested sitting around the kitchen table with your teens, not only discussing condom technique, but giving each teen both a cucumber and a condom so they could practise under the parent's supervision! I wondered how this would go over in real life so I asked a couple of teens (who, at their insistence shall remain nameless forever). Their reaction was absolute horror. I got the impression that they'd rather write a four-hour math exam than be subjected to even five minutes of such an experience. The compromise they deemed acceptable was that a box of condoms could be placed in the bathroom cabinet and they would be willing, in privacy, to practise on their own. I think this is the best deal you're likely to get out of most teens.

MATE SELECTION – Dating

It might seem a tad odd to be discussing "mate selection" and adolescents in the same paragraph, but let me continue. How many people do you know who married their "high-school sweetheart" or someone they met while still very, very young? And how many of those couples were subsequently, painfully divorced? Teens and young adults are particularly vulnerable to getting caught up in the emotional tsunami that floods their senses when they fall in love. It never occurs to them to think about their own compatibility with their lover's values and long-term goals. They probably haven't even defined what their own goals or values are, let alone compared them to their beloved's. If they do have any misgivings about any "mismatches" they've noticed, they reassure themselves that he or she "will change once we're married".

How to Influence Who Your Son or Daughter Brings Into the Family

No, you won't get veto power. The point of influence is long, long before that. Sit down with your son or daughter, before they start dating and ask them to think about the qualities and characteristics they would want in an ideal future mate. They'll probably think you're crazy, but persist in helping them tease out what it is they really hope and dream for. What qualities and characteristics will he or she have?

- Will they be world travellers in the backpack lane?
- Is a compatible religious faith important?
- How about a commitment to education and a professional career?
- Do they see themselves living a simple rural life or an upscale urban lifestyle?
- Children at 25 or 35 or never?
- Will they want someone who shares their enthusiasm for football or someone who'll play pickup guitar in their rock band?
- Are they fitness fanatics or armchair coaches?
- How do they see themselves spending their money? Building a home? Riding a Harley?

There are no right or wrong answers here and at age fourteen or fifteen your teens hopefully aren't looking for a mate. But if they get in the habit of identifying what their hopes, dreams and values are then it's more likely they will continue to think like this, and choose whether or not to date someone based on whether or not they are a "fit". Then, when at age twenty-five they "fall in love" it will be with someone they have already pre-selected to match their goals and values.

No, you won't get to choose who they bring into the family, but if you teach them how to define their own goals and values, you've given them an invaluable tool for making good choices for themselves. That's what the job of parenting is all about – giving them the tools to make good choices for themselves.

HOMOSEXUALITY

Has your teen told you they are homosexual, or are you jumping to conclusions because their friendships are all same-sex and they're not dating? Many teens show little interest in dating, usually for very healthy reasons.

> *As one teen explained, "I'm interested in girls, but from what I've seen, they just eat up your whole life. I wouldn't mind taking this girl in my chem class out once in a while, but that won't be good enough. If I ask her out for Friday night, then I have to call her on Saturday and tell her what a great time I had. And then I better ask her out again real quick or all her friends will think I've dumped her and she looks bad. So before you know it I have a "relationship" and that means I have to spend hours on the phone every night so my grades will fall . We'll end up going everywhere together so I'll have to be polite and buy her stuff and there goes all my money. There is no such thing as "casual" dating. I like to spend my time working out and rock climbing with my friends. I don't waste my money on fast food, I use it for equipment or put it in the bank for my car. In the evening I'm either doing homework or working at my job, so I don't know where I'd work in a two-hour phone call each night to a girl. So yeah, I'm interested in girls alright, but I don't have the time or the money for them right now."*

Girls, usually the more mature ones, have their own reasons for not wanting to date, but in their case the reasoning most often goes something like, "I would like to date but all the guys in my school are immature dorks." And since girls often do mature a few years earlier than boys, her assessment of the field may, indeed, be true from her perspective!

Teens often form very tight attachments to same-sex friends. They may also absolutely worship a same-sex coach, teacher or friend. It's also normal for teens to have some homosexual thoughts and feelings as their sexuality is developing. None of this means they are homosexual and premature labelling may confuse the teen who is struggling to make sense of his or her developing sexuality.

If real women are skinny and have long, straight hair, how do we fit in if we're chubby, and have hair that curls like a brillo pad?

For a teen, "exploring their sexuality" has a lot more to do with discovering how they fit into the world of men or women than it does with whether or not, or with whom, they have sexual intercourse.

Sexuality Is About a Lot More than Sex

For a teen, "exploring their sexuality" has a lot more to do with discovering how they fit into the world of men or women than it does with whether or not, or with whom, they have sexual intercourse.

Society in general, and we as parents, have sent them lots of messages about what real men or real women are. Sometimes these messages don't fit with who the teen sees in his or her own mirror. For instance, if real men are tall and have hairy legs, how do we fit in if we're short and hairless? If real women are skinny but big-breasted and have long, straight hair, how do we fit in if we're chubby, small-breasted and have hair that curls like a brillo pad?

These are just the exterior features. What about the internal attitudes and emotions that so many of us find just don't fit the norm? We're just not "one of the guys" or "one of the girls" when it comes to fitting in attitudinally or emotionally. What if we're a guy but we don't like sports, or a girl who doesn't care about clothes? At a time in their lives when they are already insecure about themselves, confusion about where they fit into the world of men and women is normal. No wonder teens can get moody and uncommunicative. They've got a lot to figure out.

Most of us grow up with a clear sense that we are heterosexual. Although scientists are starting to find clues in our genes, why some of us are homosexual is still pretty much a mystery. We do know, however, that it's not an illness or a hormone imbalance or because their parents did a bad job. There is nothing we can do to influence our child's sexual orientation – it's pre-ordained at birth. Even so, society doesn't make life easy for homosexuals, so if our son or daughter does declare themselves to be homosexual, they especially need our acceptance. Being open and available to discussion and making home a place they belong and feel safe, is very important.

It is normal to experience real heartache at discovering your child is homosexual.

As a parent, though, it is normal to experience real heartache at discovering your child is homosexual. We know how cruel and difficult the world can be and declaring yourself homosexual guarantees a rougher passage. Homophobia, especially during the high school years is rampant, and homosexual teens have to make very difficult choices. Because sexuality is about so much more than who we have sex with, denying sexuality means living a lie about so much of who we really are. Teens with inner integrity find it very, very difficult to live this kind of charade. On the other hand, declaring their sexuality can be a very dangerous thing for teens to do. How dangerous depends on the milieu within which they live, but it can range from exclusion and destroyed friendships, to lost job opportunities, to beatings and in some cases, has even led to death. To get the kind of assistance parents need to support their homosexual teen and help them build a happy and fulfilling life, parents need to look beyond the traditional sources of parenting advice and seek out organizations that specifically support homosexual teens and their parents. In small towns and rural areas, finding such organizations will require more sleuthing. Check the internet, library directories, or call the Information Services of the nearest large city. How we view homosexuality – indeed how we view anyone who is different – these views are changing, unfortunately not quickly enough. Make home the one place your teen is absolutely certain of acceptance and love.

~ Chapter Six ~

ALCOHOL, TOBACCO, AND OTHER DRUGS
Making Abuse Unlikely

You cannot guarantee that your teens won't abuse alcohol and other drugs, but you can make it much less likely. Teens with low self-esteem and a lack of courage, both for facing their own problems and resisting peer pressure, are the most vulnerable to drug use. Fortunately, parents have a great deal of influence in these areas.

Value your kids and they will value themselves. More than anything else, this is the underlying theme of this whole book. Teens who value themselves don't do things to hurt themselves. They might take a few tokes here or there, or get into a parent's liquor cabinet and water down the vodka, but they don't systematically and continuously abuse their bodies with alcohol and other drugs.

Valuing your children means listening to them and taking their opinions into account; it means asking them for advice in their areas of expertise, then taking it. It means spending time with them one-on-one, especially during those younger years when they are eager for our company. It means being available to chauffeur them around, watching their soccer game on rainy Saturday mornings, taking our lunch to work so we can pay for their math tutor, and giving up the family room so they can have some privacy with their friends. It means teaching children how to make good decisions for themselves by giving them lots of practice in

Promote the idea that they are the best person to make decisions for themselves. Only wusses and total idiots let people of lesser intelligence make their decisions for them.

decision making and learning from their own mistakes. It means expressing confidence in their own ability to take care of themselves, even when we're scared to death for them.

When our teens walk out the door each morning, they are on their own. We cannot hold their hand all the way to school or be there at lunch when "everyone" is smoking dope behind the backstop. We won't be there on Friday night when someone pulls out a bottle, and we won't be there on Sunday afternoon when the kids are doing cocaine at the mall. The only person who can keep our teen safe is him or herself.

Promote the idea that they are smart and that they are the best person to make decisions for themselves. Only wusses and total idiots let other people make decisions for them. They are smarter than the people they hang out with at school. They should be making their own decisions for themselves, not letting someone of lesser intelligence do it for them.

Of course, if you want this kind of thinking to become a natural part of themselves, you will have to honour the decisions they make for themselves in other areas of their lives too. Rather than point-blank telling them what to do, teach them to make well-thought-out decisions by:
- brainstorming options and
- exploring the consequences of each one.

Finish by expressing confidence in their ability to choose the best option for themselves. And realize that more and more often, your teen will know, much better than you, what is best for them. Honour that.

BUT I'M THE PARENT!

Yes, you are the parent and there are times when it is appropriate to step in. Realize, however, that parental "control" is an illusion. We can influence our teens but when they walk out the door they will do what they decide is best for themselves. But there is much that we can do.

Educate Yourself

If you don't know the facts, you will lose credibility. Kids get all kinds of information about alcohol and other drugs in classes at school, so they've heard the facts. Make sure you are at least as knowledgable. Contact your local drug education service for pamphlets, booklets, or programs. Also become aware of what resources are available in your community for those teens who do develop a problem. If you won't need this information for your family, you will certainly know another parent who'll need to know.

Define Your Own Values

Give some thought to your own values around alcohol, tobacco, and other drugs. If you have a partner, talk about it. You don't have to agree about everything but you will have to present a common front where the kids are concerned. Ask yourself questions like:

- How, where, why do I use alcohol and what behaviour am I modelling?
- Do I drink and drive?
- Is it "okay" to drink and drive after two beer but not after four?
- Do we have champagne or wine "to celebrate" the big events in our lives?
- Am I against them having any alcohol ever, just until they are of legal age, or what?
- Is a beer at home okay but sneaking into bars not okay?
- Will I pick them up anywhere, anytime if they've been drinking?

How do I feel about my kids smoking and doing other drugs?
- No drugs never, ever?
- Prescription drugs and aspirin are okay? When?
- Marijuana is okay but heroin is a definite "no"?

How will you answer their questions about your own alcohol and other drug use during your own youth? Lying is not a good option.

Establish Tolerances and Consequences

Every family has to decide, for themselves, what tolerances and consequences will be observed in their family. The important thing is that these are thought through, clearly stated, and enforced. It is also important that this discussion happens long before the issue of alcohol and other drug use becomes personal. When your teen comes home drunk or stoned is not the time to *start* developing policy. You'll be too emotional and your teen will be on the defensive.

When your teen comes home drunk or stoned is not the time to start developing policy.

Use movies, magazine articles, and news stories to bring up issues around alcohol and other drug use. Explore your teen's attitudes with them and stay open-minded to their point of view. Discuss issues with respect and a willingness to hear them out. Make sure you know what you're talking about and remember that this is an issue of influence, not control. You can and should establish the standards of behaviour in your own home, but you cannot control what happens once your teens walk out the door. By staying calm, credible, and respectful of them you become more influential in their lives.

After defining your values and exploring your teen's attitudes, think about what behaviour you will tolerate and what you will not; then decide on what the consequences will be.

> For example, one family has a "no use" rule that is clearly stated, understood by everyone, and applies to everyone in their home, both teen and adult. The consequence of breaking this rule would be that the teen or adult gives up driving the car for a period of time.

> Another family has a more tolerant approach and states that up to two beer or two glasses of wine, drunk in a home setting, with no driving involved is okay. Smoking is okay in the yard, but not in the house. Other drugs, however, are not tolerated and the consequence of breaking these rules is that the teen's allowance is withdrawn (because the parents choose not to be paying for their teen's drugs).

Only you (and your child's other parent) will know what is right for your family. The important thing is that you think the issues through, talk to your kids about them, clearly state your tolerances and the consequences involved, and then be consistent in enforcing them.

Model a Drug-Free Lifestyle

We live in a society that reaches for drugs to solve every problem:

- Have a stress headache? Take a pill instead of dealing with the stress.
- Have high blood pressure? We could probably do a lot to alleviate this through diet and exercise, but why bother when we can take a pill?
- Have heartburn? Take medication and keep eating whatever we want.
- Feeling depressed? Why deal with it when pills can make us happy?

We are bombarded with commercials and advertisements that tell us that, for every problem, there is a drug solution.

One of the major reasons kids do drugs is to escape from problems. Teach them, through your own example, that problems have solutions. There will always be occasions when medication is the only answer, but make it the *last* thing you try instead of the first. Empower your teens to confront and resolve their own problems without drugs. Be their role model.

> *The later kids start smoking, drinking, or trying other drugs, the less likely it is that these activities will move to the addictive and abusive level.*

Delaying First Use

Research shows that the later kids start smoking, drinking, or trying other drugs, the less likely it is that these activities will move from the experimental to the addictive and abusive level. Many alcohol, tobacco, and other drug prevention programs now base their work on this premise. "Delaying first use" is a valuable strategy, particularly because, while it is during those very early teen years when abusive behaviour first gets rooted, it's during those same years that parents generally still have a lot of control over their children's activities. These are the years to make sure they are busy playing soccer and hockey, taking ballet lessons, and going to summer camps. During these early teen years it's usually relatively easy to be a strong presence in their lives, coaching their sports teams, going hiking together, playing cards in the evening,

Anyone who still thinks parenting kids is something they can schedule into their day-timer for seven o'clock on Tuesday nights is going to lose their kids here.

doing their homework with them, and taking them camping and swimming and biking and to the movies. Anyone who still thinks parenting kids is something they can schedule into their daytimer for seven o'clock on Tuesday nights and call it "quality time" is going to lose their kids here. Parenting is a hands-on job.

Somewhere along the way most kids will pick up their first beer or smoke their first cigarette. If it happens at seventeen, as opposed to twelve, they'll be much better equipped to evaluate the experience and decide how they want to handle it. That's why "delaying first use" is worth working at.

Teach Refusal Skills

Some teens have such a strong sense of themselves that they've no problem just saying "No" and getting respect for it. Others need a little help learning how to say "No" in a way that lets them off the hook with their friends, but doesn't mean they'll be ostracized.

Role play scenarios with them, having them play the part of the kid who is offering the alcohol/drugs. They will know the kind of language and tactics these kids use to pressure their peers. You play the part of your kid, offering responses like the following:

- *I don't think so, I get really sick when I drink.*
- *Someone has to stay straight and see that you get home okay.*
- *I'm allergic to it.*
- *My Mom/Dad can smell dope from twenty miles away. I'll be grounded for ten years!*
- *Hey, I wanna have fun and I'll miss all the action if I'm drunk/stoned.*
- *Nah, I act too stupid when I'm drunk/stoned.*
- *Don't waste your stuff on me, I'll just barf it all up.*

Looking for work is something that we all find difficult. Be waiting for them, when they come out and need encouragement.

Then show them how to offer an attractive alternative:
- *Why don't we go shoot some baskets instead?*
- *I'd rather go get a pizza, wanna come?*
- *I got a new video game last week. Wanna come over and play?*

Keep Them Busy

Bored kids get into trouble. It's not that simple, but "busy" certainly does help. In terms of the kinds of activities, it's important that you listen to what your kids want to do, whether it is team sports, gymnastics, body

*If they're not into physical
risks, they may need to take
psychological risks.*

building, skiing, dancing, art classes, music lessons or whatever. Be sensitive to what their interests are and help them find ways to pursue them. If money is a problem, look for ways around that. Many sports organizations, recreation centres, and fine arts institutions will waive fees for families who cannot pay, but you must ask. Your teen certainly won't do the asking, so you pick up the phone and do it.

Many teens thrive on risk-taking activities, so much so, that many treatment and rehabilitation programs are actually built on these activities. Help your teen find ways to pursue an interest in snowboarding or mountain biking or rock climbing. If they're not into physical risks, they may need to take psychological risks. Help this kind of teen explore drama clubs, dance troupes, computer programming and volunteer opportunities for activities that will stretch their abilities and potential.

Once they're old enough, a part-time job is a great way to keep them busy and out of trouble. Research has shown that teenagers who work up to fourteen hours per week actually do better in school. This is likely because, with less time, they learn to priorize their time, work on assignments ahead of time, and plan their lives better. Get a book from the library on resume writing and help your teen write one. Talk about what kind of environment they would like to work in: gas station, restaurant, child care, swimming pool, retail store, construction site, and so on. Help them focus their job search on those areas where they would be most happy. Talk to them about what employers look for and prepare them for interview situations by role playing. Then drive them around to likely places of employment so they can make in-person enquiries. They could take the bus or drive themselves, but looking for work is something that we all find difficult and hard on the ego. Be in the car, waiting for them, when they come out and need some words of encouragement.

DETECTION

What if you think there's a problem? Do you have a right to search your teen's room and belongings? I think it's helpful to use the same criteria the police have for executing search warrants. They must have "probable cause" to search; meaning that they can't just think someone might be concealing drugs, they have to have some concrete evidence to go on. Be cautious about this, because once you start invading your teen's privacy, it dramatically and negatively changes the relationship between you. Use this invasion of their privacy as a last resort.

> *One of the best methods of monitoring your teen's behaviour is to simply be there when they come home.*

One of the best ways you have of monitoring your teen's behaviour is to simply be there when they come home after being out with friends. Are they incoherent or acting suspiciously? Do they smell of alcohol, strong breath mints, or incense? Will they look you in the eye and carry on a normal conversation? Are their pupils dilated? Your own instincts are your best detection device.

Also, be aware that drug use generally causes significant changes in a teen's behaviour. The following are warning signs:

- *An A student becomes a C student, a C student becomes an E student.*
- *Their appearance and personal hygiene deteriorates.*
- *They stop doing activities they formerly enjoyed.*
- *A formerly hard-working student doesn't complete assignments, misses school, sleeps in a lot.*
- *Teens on drugs get into trouble at school, at home, and with the law because of vandalism, fighting, and so on.*
- *They become reluctant to bring friends home or there is a marked change in the type of kids they hang out with.*

On their own, none of the above are absolute indicators of drug use, but a parent should be alert to patterns of changing behaviour. If you are concerned that your child is using alcohol and/or other drugs, contact your local drug education service for information about how to confront your teen and deal with the problem. You will need the help and support of others to do this. You are not alone.

*If your boat is still doing donuts in the marina,
the family council will get your oars pulling in the
same direction.*

~ Chapter Seven ~

THE HOMEFRONT

A Place Where Everyone's Needs are Respected

The difference between families in distress and those in which everyone thrives is not the presence or absence of problems, but how those problems are handled. As a family matures and the children become adolescents, how the family functions comes under stress. Teens start straining for independence, for the right to do things their way. Because of where they are in their development, teens are almost totally self-absorbed and usually see things only as they themselves are affected. Their parents, however, look at how things affect the whole family and demand that their teens show sensitivity to the needs of every member of the family. Both parents and teens want the teens to grow up, but they have very different ideas of how that should happen.

The difference between families in distress and those in which everyone thrives is not the presence or absence of problems, but how those problems are handled.

It's as if everyone can see Paradise Island up ahead, but each member of the family has a different map for getting there. Since family members share the same boat, however, these differences present a navigational challenge that must be successfully negotiated if everyone is going to progress peacefully to Paradise!

THE FAMILY COUNCIL ...Democracy In Action

The family council is one way of getting everyone's oar pulling in the same direction. Each member of the family has a voice in running the "family business" and they learn how to pull together as a team, toward goals they've set together. A family council is democracy in action, so if you're still stuck on the idea that you know best and everything will be fine once everyone just starts doing what you tell them to do, then read no further. However, if you've already tried that and your boat is still doing donuts in the marina, you're ready for the family council.

The family council is a time and place when each member of the family is heard with respect and both the perks and the problems of the family are shared and dealt with by everyone. With some guidance, family members can learn:

- responsibility – as they make choices that the whole family will have to live with;
- courage – when they disagree with others but choose to speak up anyway;
- how to express themselves in language that doesn't make others defensive;
- that everyone has reasons for doing what they do;
- that some problems take time to resolve; and
- how to function in a democracy.

How To Get Started

1. Set a day and time for the first meeting when family members will be able to attend.
2. Invite everyone who lives in your household to attend. If everyone won't come, fine. Start with those who will. Never try to force participation.
3. Make the first meeting short and pleasant. Use it to plan an enjoyable activity, explain how a family council works and set the agenda for the next meeting.

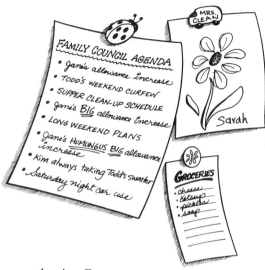

Ground Rules

1. Every person has an equal voice. Even a very young child will have good ideas and must be able to speak with confidence. Absolutely no put-downs are permitted.

2. Everyone should share what they think or feel about each issue. If someone doesn't want to talk, that's okay. Just being present is inclusive and will help make everyone feel that they're part of the process.

3. Decisions are made by consensus. This doesn't mean that the final decision is everyone's first choice; that would be impossible. It does mean that the result is a decision that everyone can live with.

4. All decisions will be in effect until the next family council.

5. Some decisions are reserved for parents to make, but discussion must always be encouraged. For example, if a parent's job has been transferred and the family has to move, this will not usually be a decision the family as a whole can make. However, the whole family should express their feelings about it and be actively involved in planning the move.

6. There are two "positions" and these should revolve among all the family members capable of carrying them out. The chairperson keeps the discussion on track and makes sure that each person's opinion is heard and considered. The secretary keeps notes about the decisions made, writes them up as minutes, and reads them at the next meeting.

> *Decisions are made by consensus. This doesn't mean that the final decision is everyone's first choice; that would be impossible. It does mean that the result is a decision that everyone can live with.*

Encourage Input

Write "Agenda" on a piece of paper, tape it to the fridge each week, and invite everyone to contribute. This is a good way to temporarily shelve frustrating problems until they can be dealt with calmly by all members at the family council. When kids know that at the family council meeting they will get a fair hearing, they become more willing to shelve their disputes until then. Another advantage, of course, is that by the time the family council meeting comes, the hot and heavy emotions that were part of their dispute will mostly have dissipated and the problem can be dealt with much more calmly.

Setting the Agenda

When planning the agenda for family council, include the following:
- *Compliments* - an opportunity to show appreciation for special efforts. Parents will probably have to take the lead in this for a while. Throughout the week try to take note of any special deeds that should be complimented. These compliments need to be for exceptional effort and they need to be meaningful. Consequently some weeks a family member will be complimented, other weeks not.
- *Minutes* – read the last meeting's minutes.
- *Old Business* – unfinished topics and unresolved issues from the last meeting.
- *Finances* – a good time to hand out allowances or discuss purchases.
- *New Business* – plan for the future (holidays are always a good topic) and deal with complaints and problems.

Problems and Complaints

Encourage your kids to put their problems and complaints on the agenda for family council meetings. Using the following, step-by-step process to resolve these conflicts will help keep these "discussions" from becom-

Creative Conflict Resolution Process

1. Ask the person with the complaint to explain the problem. Do not interrupt them. After they've explained it, ask them, "Is this still a problem?"

2. If it is, ask anyone else involved to explain their point of view. They shouldn't be interrupted while they are speaking. After they've finished, anyone present may ask clarifying questions.

3. Have everyone brainstorm solutions, with someone (the secretary if this is at a family council meeting) writing down all the ideas. At this point no one should comment on whether the ideas are good, bad or even possible.

4. Read through all the ideas that have been recorded, then discuss each one, respectfully exploring the pros and cons of each idea.

5. Through discussion, arrive at a decision that everyone can live with. The secret to successful conflict resolution is realizing that the solution isn't likely to be everyone's first choice, but it is a solution everyone can live with.

6. If the family simply cannot come to a resolution there are two options: table the issue until a future family council meeting (emotions might still be too high for successful resolution) or have the parent(s) impose a decision. The last option (parent imposes decision) should only be used as an absolute last resort, as it is the least effective way to solve a problem.

7. Put the decision into action. It will stay in effect until at least the next family council when the family should evaluate how things have gone.

ing a useless free-for-all!

The family council will not solve all of a family's problems, but it will go a long way toward getting all those oars pulling in the same direction. Establishing the habit of family council meetings in your family is relatively easy when kids are pre-teen and even during those early years of adolescence. If you're reading this and your kids are already fifteen or sixteen years old it may be harder. Every family has to decide if the effort is worth it for them, but I would strongly urge you to give family council meetings a good try. Don't insist your teens attend, but serve notice about what is on the agenda for the meeting (post the agenda, being sure to list at least one or two items in which they have a vested interest. For example: allowance review; summer holidays; curfew review; Christmas present budget; car use schedule.) and that decisions will be made at the meeting even if the only person who attends is Mom. When they do show up, make sure their views are listened to and seriously given consideration. Family council meetings cannot ever become just a facade. Kids have to feel like they definitely have some power in these discussions.

A single parent without other adult back-up can be overwhelmed by the sheer energy and verbal volume from teens who see everything as being on the table for discussion. This can wear a parent out. These parents have suggested that holding the same kinds of discussions, but in the presence of a family counsellor who helps maintain the power balance, is very helpful. Very often the counsellor is only needed to get the family started on the right track. After that they can be a resource for mediating only particularly contentious issues.

HOUSE RULES ...Are For Everyone

As a parent, make a clear distinction between those things in your home life which are negotiable and those that are not. For example, foul language and smoking indoors may be non-negotiable, while telephone time and chores are negotiable. At a family council meeting, discuss those distinctions and together, with your kids, agree on the consequences of breaking the non-negotiable rules. Once that is settled (and recorded), turn your attention to the negotiable items and invite discussion about how the family would like to see them handled.

The purpose of house rules is to make "home" a place where everyone truly belongs. It should be a place where everyone's needs for priva-cy, peace, support, and recreation are met. Rules make sure that one per-son's needs aren't being met at the expense of someone else's.

> *For Example: When Jan's mom comes home from work, she really needs peace and quiet for an hour or two. Although she likes Jan's friends and doesn't really have a problem with the music, she just can't handle coming home every night to a house full of teenagers and the stereo thumping out their boom-da-da-boom music at full blast. Jan was really embarrassed when her Mom would come home at 6:00 and totally lose her cool in front of her friends.*

> *Once they talked about it and agreed that Mom's need for peace after work and Jan's need to have friends over were both legitimate, they came up with a plan. Jan can have her friends over and her music as loud as she wants until 5:45 each day. Then Jan herself throws her friends out and turns off her music. After 7:30 in the evening she can have a maximum of two friends over, but the volume on the stereo can't crank past "3". She is also allowed to have as many friends over as she likes on Saturdays but Sundays are "quiet" days.*

> *For Example: In the Patterson home things were a little different. During dinner Dad liked to turn on the kitchen television and watch the news. Other family members found this really disruptive. After Dad realized how much the family wanted his company (and not just the back of his head), he agreed to tape the news or watch the late evening news instead. Other alternatives the family had consid-ered in their discussion were eating dinner an hour before the news (rejected because everyone wouldn't be home yet) or an hour after (Dad said he was too hungry to wait that long).*

In homes where parents make all the rules, they are also required to be the police. Combine this autocratic rule-making and enforcement with the intense push for independence that's part of a teen's natural development and you have a home that quickly becomes a battleground for power. It's not a pleasant place for anyone, especially not parents.

If everyone can step back and look at the issue of house rules with the perspective that rules exist to make sure everyone's needs are met, it's only natural that the whole family would be involved in defining them.

When everyone is part of the process and the rules are accepted as being in everyone's best interest, then everyone also shares in enforcement.

Good Enough For Us Standards

When we don't really think things through, we often parent on automatic pilot – the way we were parented. Similarly, we often base our housekeeping standards on those of our parent's households. But a lot has changed. Those standards may no longer fit our lifestyle.
Sit down with your family and develop "good enough for us standards". Start by drawing up a list of the housekeeping chores that each of you feels must be done.

For example:
- *cleaning the bathroom*
- *making beds*
- *buying groceries*
- *paying the bills*
- *mowing the lawn*
- *washing windows*

Priorize each chore.
For example:
- *Buying groceries might be an "A" list item – everyone agrees this must be done in order for them to eat.*
- *Cleaning the bathroom might be a "B" list item – should be done.*
- *Making beds might be a "C" list item – no one will die if this gets missed.*

Next, look at how often these things need to be done.
For example:
- *Maybe washing windows could happen twice a year instead of once a month.*
- *Maybe it's only necessary to make beds when sheets are changed.*
- *Maybe with a little more planning grocery shopping could happen every two weeks instead of every week.*

Once you've come up with your family's "good enough for us" standards, talk about how you're going to accomplish the work you've all agreed needs to be done.

For example:
- *Are members willing to negotiate who'll do what or should a "draw" system be used?*
- *How often should the new system be evaluated and chores re-allocated?*
- *Is the family willing to give up something else to pay someone to do some of these tasks?*

There are a lot of reasons why, for women particularly, the process of handing over control of housekeeping standards described above can be very difficult. Many of us have, ourselves, been raised in homes where we were taught that what differentiated a "good" home from "trash" were the housekeeping standards. But very few parents are full-time homemakers anymore and these standards are no longer realistic. Most of us would also like to think that our value is based on abilities other than our housekeeping but I know we haven't all made that evolutionary leap yet!

But housekeeping standards themselves are evolving. My grand-mother would never have served store-bought bread. She set aside one whole day each week for baking the family's bread and rolls. My mother

I like the style of one family – they've nailed a sign to their front door that reads: "We choose to have a messy house!"

tells me that during the first years of her marriage, she ironed everything - sheets, towels, underwear, diapers, socks, etc. During my own early years of homemaking, my Saturday house cleaning was so thorough that I turned out and re-arranged every drawer in our bedroom, every week.

But now, twenty years later, I don't have a single guilty thought about serving store-bought bread. I can't remember when I last turned out a drawer and even my mother quit ironing underwear thirty years ago!

Sharing the responsibility for setting and maintaining housekeeping standards can be very difficult, but once you've made that leap and had a few months to get used to the new way of doing things, there can be an incredible sense of liberation. It's definitely worth it. I like the style of one family I heard about – they've nailed a sign to their front door that reads: "We choose to have a messy house!"

There will be other times in our lives, tidier times when there are no schoolbooks on the table or jackets flung over the couch. That conglomeration of shoes at the back door will have disappeared and there'll be no wet towels on the bathroom floor. And we'll remember these "messy" days of our lives as the *best* days of our lives and wonder why we fussed so much. So review your standards and explore why you are actually doing some of the things you do.

One mother told me that she had been resenting the hours she spent folding her teenage kids' laundry. When she brought it up at a family council meeting, the kids told her to stop folding. According to them, they stuffed it helter-skelter into their drawers and didn't worry about creases because every morning they just used the "stick-it-in-the-dryer-for-five-minutes" method of "ironing" their clothes. It took her a few tries to get past the feeling that she wasn't quite doing her job as a mother, but she managed.

Everyone needs to be master of their own domain.

Which brings us to another subject that seems to cause a lot of grief in homes – the kids' bedrooms. Parents! Let go of this! This isn't your room. Everyone needs to be master of their own domain. You have every right to insist that they keep the door shut, but keep your nose out of their bedroom. They may go months without picking the clothes off the floor or changing the sheets, but they probably won't. Once it's no longer a battleground between you, they'll probably keep it in much better shape. And if they don't, don't worry about it – they live in it. You don't have to. If you're worried about insect or rodent infestation, insist on a no-food rule in bedrooms, but otherwise, just insist they keep the door shut!

In most families, different members have different standards. Those differences happen between couples and it's a given that they happen between siblings. In one family, two brothers shared a bathroom and of course one was a neat freak and one was a pig. Naturally, the pig drove the neat freak crazy and the neat freak thought the pig was just being a pig to make him crazy (which some of the time was no doubt true). In a family council meeting they each listed their complaints about the other, then priorized them. Then they went through the list, coming to agreement on what was intolerable and what each could live with. For example, the neat freak could not tolerate the pig leaving his underwear on the floor. The pig agreed to use the hamper if the neat freak would quit whining about the toilet paper roll sitting on the counter instead of being installed on the dispenser. The neat freak readily agreed that he would willingly put the toilet paper roll in the dispenser without ever whining again if he never had to pick up another piece of the pig's underwear! Their resolution was not either's first choice, but they came to an agreement that both could live with!

Be Flexible

Be flexible about how much you expect your teens to do. Chores need to be in proportion to their other activities. That said, teens also need to be depended upon. They need to be needed, to be making an essential contribution to their family life. Fifty or sixty years ago, children were genuinely needed by their families. Without their efforts the family might not survive, literally. While this might

If our teen's only contact with organizing a meal is walking up to a counter and saying "I'll have fries with that", then we are not doing our job.

have been too heavy a burden for them, today's world in which a teen comes home to a house where all the housekeeping tasks have already been done by a maid service (or his overworked, stressed-out parent), makes them redundant. They aren't needed and we all need to be needed.

Several other issues should be considered here as well. One is the responsibility of a parent to ensure that their child can look after themselves in the world. If our teen's only contact with organizing a meal is walking up to a counter and saying "I'll have fries with that", then we are not doing our job. Teens need to learn how to put together a nutritious meal, do laundry without ruining clothes, and clean up a bathroom. It is our job as parents to ensure that they have the skills they need to take care of themselves, and most of us learn best by doing.

Second, there is the issue of cleaning up our own dirt. When all the cleaning is done by a service (usually a woman), children and teens come to the elitist opinion that this is somehow beneath them. When I picked

*Agree with them.
Cleaning the toilet is gross and you
hate it too. But they aren't doing it
because they like it, they are doing it
because it needs to be done.*

up on this attitude with my own kids (around ages eleven or twelve), the regular cleaning service got cancelled. There is no doubt our house is messier but while they are teens, they are learning to clean up their own dirt. It plays a big part in keeping us all in touch with reality.

Agree on an area of responsibility for your teens (like making dinner once a week or doing the laundry), then back off. They can handle it. Maybe not as neatly or quickly or cleverly as you, but they can handle it.

Finally, we all hate chores. Teens especially hate chores. Being part of the process that determined the "good enough for us" standards will help control the grumbling but it won't eliminate it. As a parent, accept that.

They will complain about chores and if they're having a bad day they may even need to slam a door. What they don't need is some parent trying to convince them that it really isn't that bad. For them it is that bad. When a teen starts in with their "poor me" and "this is so gross" lament, don't argue with them. Agree with them. Cleaning the toilet *is* gross and you hate it too. They aren't doing it because they like it, they are doing it because it *needs* to be done. Then get out of their way because most of the grouching is for your benefit.

SIBLING RIVALRY

Fighting ...it's communication and it's entertainment.

When most of us first contemplated having a second child, we envisioned loving children playing happily together. As they grew up, we imagined that they'd be best buddies, protecting and sticking up for each other. It would be them against the world. Considering that most of us grew up in families with siblings with whom we fought constantly, it's amazing that this fantasy persists. We should know better.

The truth is, there are calm and happy moments. There are times when they stick up for each other and when there are crises, they usually do come through, but in the meantime, the reality is that siblings love to fight. It's part of the dialogue of growing up. It's communication and it's entertainment. Kids seem to love it. Parents hate it. There is nothing more likely to drive a parent over the edge than a couple of kids nattering at each other, day after day after day. Fortunately, there are some things you can do.

Understanding Sibling Rivalry

Although fighting does take on a life of its own over the years, the roots of sibling rivalry are not in your kids' relationship with each other, but in their relationship with you. From birth they have looked to you to provide everything they needed and in their own little universe, they were the centre. The first child stayed in that universe for several years – until the second child came along. The second child probably only had a few months of such bliss before she looked around and noticed that there was someone else competing for your attention too. From the beginning, each of them wanted you to love them and them alone. They did not want to share you.

Parents can do a lot during the second pregnancy and in those first few months to smooth the way for a more peaceful sibling relationship. But if you're reading this book now, you're no doubt long past those opportunities, so we'll skip past them to what you can do now.

Set the Stage for Peace
Understanding the sources of sibling rivalry and realizing that competition for your attention is still a major motivation (or at least habit!) helps us look at how our behaviour as parents can affect sibling warfare.

1. Eliminate Comparisons
Keeping in mind that competition for your attention is at the root of most sibling rivalry, eliminate comparisons from your vocabulary. The most obvious, of course, are statements like, "Why can't you be neat like your brother?" Less obvious, but equally as powerful in their negative effects, are comparisons that are designed to make one child feel better about himself. For example, "Wow, you sure did a great job of painting that picture. I'm sure your sister can't do anything like that." A comment like this is meant well, but it reinforces the belief that you, as the parent, are measuring them against each other.

2. Value Differences
Encourage your kids to pursue their own interests and have their own friends. After spending a fortune on hockey equipment for their oldest son it's natural for parents to want the second son to follow in the same sport (using all the stuff the old one has grown out of), but we mustn't expect it. If the second son is more inclined to music and really wants a guitar, we need to be prepared to honour that and make an investment in a guitar. If money is going to be a problem, don't blow the bank on the first son. Shop for used hockey equipment so that there'll be something for second son too. Encourage your kids to have part-time jobs and earn their own equipment. Similarly, honour your kids' rights to have friends of their own. Don't try to force one kid to include the other, just because the second one is lonely or bored or has no friends of his own. Instead,

Promote the idea that in a family,
"fair" is a long-term kind of thing.
Encourage the meeting of needs.

work with the second child to find out what's going on and help them get involved in activities that will develop their own set of friends.

3. Give Up Labels

Think for a moment about what labels say: the big guy, the smart one, the messy one, the lazy one, the slowpoke, or the sensitive one are common examples. Labels like these categorize people and as a society we attach a lot of baggage to them. They define us and, too often, are self-fulfilling. Thus, "the baby of the family" grows up to be irresponsible and dependent on family to bail her out of bad decisions. Labels also exclude others. For example, if daughter number one is "the math genius", does this mean daughter number two is stupid? Avoid labels in favour of simply using their given names. Thus, I would introduce my daughter as, "This is my daughter, Lorie," not, "This is Lorie, the baby of the family."

4.   Fair Doesn't Mean Equal

Sometimes parents bend over backwards trying so hard to be fair to their kids that, in fact, the whole family suffers.

> *For Example: Dad, who works in an auto-body shop, gets an opportunity to buy a motor scooter for $200. The engine is great. All the scooter needs is body work, which Dad and Josh could do on weekends. Dad knows Josh would love it and it would be a good project for the two of them. He feels bad about not having anything for Trina, so he gives her a cheque for two hundred dollars, which she blows on clothes. A few months later Trina gets an opportunity to go on a ski trip with her school. It costs $350 so to make up for it to Josh, Dad gets him the leather jacket he's been whining for. And on the story goes. The family gets ever more deeply into debt and the kids are unhappy that the family can't afford to go on holidays that summer.*

At her teenage son's urging, one middle-aged, out-of-shape mother started working out with him at the gym.

Promote the idea that in a family, "fair" is a long-term kind of thing. Sometimes one member will come into a great benefit and another time someone else will. Encourage the meeting of *needs*. As a parent, you may want to keep a private tally of benefits in your head, but keep this kind of calculation out of daily life. So if you're out shopping and you see the perfect shirt for Jason, go ahead and take it home. Another time, it will be Sarah's turn.

5. Time Alone
Children need time alone with their parents. Once they are teens, managing time alone together can be a little harder than when they were children

who wanted you to perch on the edge of their bed each night for story time, but it's just as important. Look for activities that both you and your teen genuinely would like to share. At her teenage son's urging, one middle-aged, out-of-shape mother started working out with him at the gym. Another parent discovered that while her daughter responded to any kind of questioning by shutting down, she loved to eat out and would happily babble away in the relaxing atmosphere of a favourite restaurant. The parent considered this once-a-week ritual to be money very well spent. Be creative and look for genuine areas of common interest to share.

6. Have Clear Rules

In your family council meetings, be clear about which house rules around behaviour are non-negotiable in your home. For example: name calling, hitting, pushing, punching, pinching, or grabbing, are usually non-negotiable. Also agree on clear rules for taking each other's belongings. If the owner's permission is required, agree in advance on a consequence for breaking this rule. What about damage to goods? If Jen scratches Jamie's cd does she have to pay to replace it? What if the cd was already two years old? It's always a bad idea to make rules in the heat of anger, so use your family council meetings as a time when the whole family brainstorms these issues and sets family policy. Then put it all in writing!

7. Keep the Responsibility on the Kids

Firmly insist that kids take responsibility for their own behaviour. John didn't call Shelly a bitch because she *made* him do it. He did it because *he* decided to.

Your kids will try to deflect responsibility onto each other, onto their teachers, onto the size of their bedrooms, and even onto you. I well remember one of my sons defiantly declaring, "It's not my fault. You're supposed to be the big expert on raising teenagers. If you did a better job of raising me, I wouldn't be this way!" Take a deep breath and firmly insist that they take responsibility for their own behaviour.

What children of any age would really, really like, would be for the parent to just make their sibling disappear. Abracadabra - POOF!

DEALING WITH FIGHTING

What children of any age would really, really like, would be for the parent to just make their sibling disappear. Abracadabra - POOF! Somewhere inside (even when they're forty) they still want to be the centre of the universe. That's the root cause of most fighting.

When your children are fighting, start by acknowledging feelings. It is hard to go about your private business while your brother is kicking the bathroom door and screaming at you. It *is* difficult to share a room with a sister who has dorky friends who sit on your bed and breathe into your air.

As much as possible, use the agenda for family council meetings to record issues that need discussion and have the family as a whole develop policy in areas that are causing fighting. Allowing some time to elapse between the conflict and the resolution process dissipates the emotional heat and makes conflict much more resolvable.

But sometimes, an issue that needs to be dealt with immediately and requires you to "have a talk" with one sibling. Do so in private. At any age, kids love to get each other into trouble and will enjoy standing nearby and listening to the other one "get it". Take the fun out of "telling".

Creative Conflict Resolution

Then make sure your kids know how to resolve conflict. Teach them that things that look unresolvable usually can be resolved and a creative "win-win" can usually be worked out. Give them the example of two people fighting over an orange. There was only one orange and they both wanted it. They were fighting bitterly over the orange, each certain that they were entitled to it. It turned out though, that when they quit calling each other names and switched from fighting to resolving the conflict, they discovered that their needs were compatible. He wanted the orange for the juice, she wanted to grate the peel for muffins.

Conflict resolution is effective when we take the emphasis off "me

Conflict resolution is effective when we take the emphasis off "me versus you" and redirect it into "we versus the problem".

versus you" and redirect it into "we versus the problem". Lead your teens through the steps of the conflict resolution process outlined on page 85. Eventually, they will get the idea that this is how conflicts are handled in your family and you'll be able to say, "I know you guys can handle this yourself."

Fighting – Evaluate How Serious It Is

Squabbling

When emotions are too overheated for immediate conflict resolution, you may need to evaluate the situation, because teens can hurt each other.

Squabbling is the normal, ongoing, back-and-forth nattering that siblings do. They are trying things out on each other and flexing their self-centred little egos and frankly, having fun. It can be nerve wracking, but this is part of the repartee siblings share. Remove yourself from the scene, or get them to remove themselves. At a family council meeting, agree on a place (like the garage) where the kids can take their squabbling. We all have our individual levels of tolerance and, since the objective is to make "home" a place where everyone is comfortable, you certainly have a right to insist that they take their squabbling elsewhere. Once such a "squabbling space" is identified (away from the parent), expect a dramatic reduction in how much of it goes on. Even though they would never dream it's so, much of this squabbling is for your benefit. They are still competing to show each other up and win your undivided favour. Each one of them wants you to say that he or she is right and the other is wrong. When you remove yourself as audience the major reason for the fighting often disappears too.

They each want you to say that he or she is right and the other is wrong.

Serious Arguing

At this stage they are very angry and may need your help. Acknowledge their anger with each other and ask them to separate for a cooling-off period. Then request that they go to the squabbling space and use conflict resolution techniques to resolve this dispute. If they cannot, ask them to put the dispute on the agenda for the next family council meeting. Make it clear, serious arguing will not be tolerated inside the home.

Dangerous Fighting

When teens are actually in danger of hurting each other, a parent needs to wade in and separate them. Start with a cooling-off period for each teen in a separate room. Then ask them if the issue can be tabled to the next family council meeting. If not, and you feel they need your help, lead them through the steps of conflict resolution. However, keep this process in their control. Act as a facilitator, asking clarifying questions and record information, but have them do 99% of the brainstorming and decision making. If resolution is looks impossible at this time, tell them there are two alternatives: the dispute will be tabled for a period time (possibly to next family council meeting) or you will make a decision that they will have to live with. As much as possible, avoid the last alternative, because they really need to find their own solutions and commit to keeping them.

Parents cannot and should not even try to solve their teen's disputes for them. Our job is to give them the tools to do this themselves, by teaching and modelling the good conflict resolution skills that will give them a valuable lifelong tool to use in all their relationships.

Chapter Eight

ENGAGING THE ADOLESCENT BRAIN

Television, Movies, Computer, Video Games, Internet, Music and Educational Etceteras

SLEEPING SICKNESS and MEMORY ATROPHY

Sleeping sickness and memory atrophy are probably the most prevalent "diseases" of adolescence and they are both nurtured by parental behaviour.

In the name of being a good parent, we spend our mornings wrestling teenagers out of bed, then chase after them with lunches, homework, and jackets. When they miss the bus we drive them to school, even if that means being late for work ourselves. We can hardly wait for the day when they'll start taking responsibility for themselves and we won't have to go through this anymore.

But responsibility for themselves will not arrive like a gift-wrapped present at some pre-determined birthday. It's developed when parents back off and let teens learn how to take care of themselves. This means letting them learn from the consequences of their own actions.

Being responsible requires that they get organized about where they put their homework and hang their jacket and leave their umbrella. It means they iron their clothes and get a "permission for field trip" form signed the night before. It requires them to get up by themselves in the morning and get their butt out the door and down to the bus stop in plenty of time to catch the bus.

Why would anyone go to all that work when their parent will do it for them? Why would they get up five minutes earlier than they have to? Your voice is their alarm clock and that alarm clock doesn't even register with

Why would they get up five minutes earlier
than they have to?

their brains until they hear the level-ten screech that tells them *now* they have to get up.

Teens have all the raw brain matter they need to think these things through and they *could* remember where they put things and organize themselves to get up and out the door each morning on their own, but when parents do it all for them, their brain simply atrophies. Their "remember" cells just shrivel up like little raisins lost in the seat cushions.

Jumpstart Their Brain Matter

Buy each member of your family their own alarm clock and calmly serve notice that you are retiring as their alarm clock and memory bank. Then do it.

Anticipate the natural consequences of this action, which will be absolute chaos for several days. Your teens will be late for school, jobs, and games. They won't know where their homework, jackets, permission slips, or house keys are. And they'll blame it all on you!

Calmly serve notice that you are retiring as their alarm clock and memory bank.

How will you handle this? It's important that while you show caring concern, you stay detached from their problems and don't bail them out. Assure them that you know they are smart and capable and will handle taking care of themselves. Let them figure out how to get to their activities or explain to coaches, teachers or bosses why they missed their ride. Similarly, with homework, lunches, and uniforms, tell them that you have confidence they can get themselves organized and remember where they left their things. This is not a lie. After several days of chaos they will start to take control of their lives and their pride in themselves will mushroom.

The parent's job is not to do everything for their children, but to teach them how to take good care of themselves. Don't expect teens to take this point of view, however. They will see your withdrawal of alarm clock and memory bank services as a loss of your time and attention. They may even feel abandoned for a while. Counterbalance this loss of your attention with extra attention that is pleasurable to you both. Schedule special time with them to do things that you both genuinely enjoy, like mountain biking, movies, eating out, or shopping.

TELEVISION, MOVIES, VIDEO GAMES, and the INTERNET

Not too long ago parenting gurus devoted a lot of type space to debating the pros and cons of television. When parents look at what is available through the internet these days, television seems quite benign. Still, I know parents who do not permit television, video games, or an internet-connection in their homes. At the other extreme, there are the families where all of the above are provided, but not supervised.

Every parent must decide what is right for their own family, but it doesn't strike me that either extreme is a workable choice for most of us. The big flaw I see in a "no use policy" is that, while we have some control over what happens in our own home (when we are present), our kids live in a much bigger world. If they don't come in contact with something we find offensive at the neighbours tomorrow, they will certainly come in contact somewhere. After talking to these sheltered kids, I've come to believe that when they do finally connect, they devour the forbidden fruit ravenously and without discrimination. They have not developed the tools they need for evaluating what they are seeing, and for deciding between what is true or worthwhile spending their time on, versus what is false and just pure garbage. Teens whose use has always been unsupervised are similarly vulnerable to absorbing the values promoted by whatever they are watching.

Parents should always keep in mind that censorship is mostly an effort to "delay first contact".

When children are young, parents have both the ability to censor their exposure (to a large degree, but never absolutely) and to spend time watching movies and television with them. While doing so, parents can facilitate the development of evaluation and critiquing skills. It's also appropriate for parents to make judgements about how mature their kids are. A thirteen-year-old, for example, is probably less capable of processing and making sound judgments about some media than a seventeen-year-old. But parents should always keep in mind that censorship is mostly an effort to "delay first contact".

By the time our children have turned into adolescents, our ability to censor their exposure has considerably narrowed. We may prohibit a particular video game or movie in our own home, but it will certainly be available somewhere else. We may put netminder software on our computer to screen out objectionable web sites, but there are routes around this software and teens pass these tips around faster than the developers invent new walls to deny access.

While no parent should permit material in their home that conflicts with their values (and this includes magazines, books, music, video games, movies, or whatever), knowing that our teens' worlds extend far beyond our own property line, I believe it is more helpful to approach this subject from the perspective of encouraging the kinds of values and critical thinking skills that help teens evaluate material and reject it for themselves, when it conflicts with their values.

Movies and Television

As a parent, provide the context of reality.

Movies and television present valuable opportunities to stimulate discussion and teach kids critical thinking and evaluation skills. As a parent, provide the context of reality by pointing out that if you, for example, were to fall four stories and bounce off the roof of a car into the back of a garbage truck, you would not be in very good shape. Talk about the values portrayed by the movies you are watching and how they affect viewers. Have you ever noticed, for example, that the "homes" people on television or movies (even those working at low-paying jobs) live in usually look like they cost at least $500,000? How might this set up young people for dissatisfaction and feed the anger of inner city youth, who assume that everyone in the world but them lives like this?

What about the ease with which movie and television characters move from relationship to relationship? Wouldn't this be painful in real life? How about all those car crashes?

Most teens clam up if they think the spotlight is on them, but they can often be drawn into a discussion about a movie character's abortion, drug problem, or relationships.

What happens to real people's insurance premiums when they drive like that?

Advertising and infomercials are a great stimulus for discussions about consumeristic attitudes and truth in advertising. How do advertisers play on people's loneliness by using upbeat music and happy, beautiful people to trick viewers into thinking that buying a particular chewing gum or beverage will improve their social life? How do the infomercials for exercise videos make it seem like their program is just one big party and the buyer will have fun, fun, fun while they lose tons of weight and achieve a totally ripped body virtually without effort, not to mention have all those great new friends to do it with?

Watching movies and television together with their teens also offers parents invaluable opportunities to discuss moral issues in a non-threatening context. Most teens clam up if they think the spotlight is on them, but they can often be drawn into a discussion about a movie character's abortion, drug problem, or relationships.

Music

Ask teens to really listen to the lyrics and read the liner notes on the music they are feeding into their brains. When they know

> *When they know what the lyrics really say, are they still comfortable with the message?*

what the lyrics really say, are they still comfortable with the message? They might believe that they are mature enough to "handle" the lyrics without absorbing the values, but are they comfortable supporting a particular performer to continue producing what amounts to "hate promotion" for younger, more vulnerable listeners? It's almost a given that most teens are attracted to the "bad boys" of the music world (we were) and they will probably defend their choice just based on the premise that "parents don't understand our music". But I have noticed that once thinking teens who've developed evaluation skills understand what some performers are actually promoting through their lyrics, they lose their taste for this music.

As you can surmise, I don't get too excited about kids and their music – as long as this music is a fairly minor part of their lives. I do, however, get very concerned about the teens who spend eighteen hours a day with earphones plastered to their skull, doing nothing but absorbing the messages and the values of groups who promote hatred and violence and disrespect for each other. I have known several suicidal teens and in each case they were kids who spent hour after hour prostrate on their beds with these negative messages mainlined into their brains through earphones. Mind you, I'd be deeply concerned about any teen who spent hour after hour, day after day, prostrate on their bed. Music or no music, these are depressed kids who need their parents to pay attention and figure out what is going on in their lives.

Video and Computer Games

As I've already said, I don't believe any parent should ever have material in their home that conflicts with their own values. That stated, however,

I've never gotten too perturbed about video games because I believe that kids who have a well-rounded life with a wide variety of sports, activities, and friendships don't get fixated on one single activity like playing video games.

Kids who pursue a variety of interests are bored by sitting in front of a video screen hour after hour after hour, no matter how great the graphics. However, there are two things that I think parents do to promote this obsessive behaviour.

First of all, they are so concerned about keeping their kids physically safe that they encourage kids to stay in the house and in front of the computer screen.

For Example: It's 3:30pm on a school day and Dad calls home to make sure that twelve-year-old Paul got home safely from school. Paul is home and when Dad asks what he's doing, Paul replies that he's on the computer playing a game. Dad is relieved. With all the gang activity these days and all the drugs out there on the street, he worries about Paul being alone for three hours every afternoon. But Paul likes computer games so Dad makes sure he always buys the latest video game. He knows Paul is safe as long as he's home playing a game.

The other thing parents do is thwart their children's genuine interests. Out of sheer boredom they vegetate in front of the video screen.

For Example: Thirteen-year-old Jeremy's friends are all into mountain biking every day after school. Jeremy was too, but after breaking his arm last year his parents decided that it was too dangerous for him and have prohibited him from taking his bike off road. So Jeremy comes home every day and plays video games because his friends are all off riding the trails and there's nothing else to do. His parents have encouraged him to join an alternate sport like swimming or curling, but he's just not interested.

In my own home I didn't prohibit video games but I didn't encourage them either. The boys pooled their own money to buy the game systems and they bought their own games. These were very expensive and a lot of newspapers had to be delivered to buy a single game! On the other hand, however, I always willingly paid the registration fees for the sports or artistic activities they wanted to participate in – keeping them busy and active. As a result I noticed that every time a hot new game came out and they (or one of their friends) purchased it, there was usually an intense period of play for a week or two; then play would fall off because there were so many more interesting things to do that engaged both their minds and their bodies. Video games were never a problem.

Computers and Internet Access

There is a misconception that if kids are "on the computer" instead of "crashed in front of the tv", they are doing something worthwhile and productive. Why? It is possible to learn a great deal from television programs or from computer programs. It is also possible to waste hours and hours of their lives in these physically immobile activities that do not necessarily add anything useful to their lives and may in fact introduce a great deal that is harmful. That is true of both television and computer time.

> *There is a misconception that if kids are at the computer, they are doing something worthwhile and productive. Why?*

Too often, parents write the cheque that pays for the latest computer technology, then go off about their own business, content that they've provided their kids a leg up in the world by making this stuff accessible for them. More is required. Parents must get computer and internet savvy themselves.

Personally, I am wildly enthusiastic about the internet. It's the biggest and most interesting library, educational opportunity, networking device, and convenience ever invented. I also realize, however, that plugging into cyberspace means I open my home to opportunists and experiences I prefer to avoid. As parents, we need to understand the technology so that our kids can reap the benefits but avoid the dangers.

Wouldn't it be easier to just pull the plug in our homes? In the short term, perhaps. But computers and internet access are rapidly becoming as much a part of our world as electricity. Historically, there was a time when some people chose to avoid electricity because it was dangerous and they didn't want to deal with it. Today we couldn't conceive of life without electricity. Similarly, computer chips now run our cars, manage our money, make the furnace work, operate the telephone system, make

We are long past being able to say, "No thanks" to computer and internet technology. The only option most of us have is deciding when we are going to learn how to make the best use of this technology.

our toast come out right, and instruct the surgeon in the operating room.

Every day, several thousand more companies and organizations choose to mount information on their internet web sites. Compared to the cost of producing and mailing out directories and catalogues, mounting information on their webpage costs them virtually nothing per visitor. Many of us who use internet technology in our daily lives have come to the place where we wouldn't want to live without it. Whether I'm checking the "yellow pages", reviewing the ferry schedule to Newfoundland, researching the history of an obscure First Nations band, looking up the weather in Yosemite, ordering a birthday present, checking property tax records, researching statistics on divorce in Saskatchewan, finding suppliers for a part on my aging barbecue, or e-mailing my relatives in Europe, I personally access the internet on a daily basis. I cannot imagine my life or work without it anymore. Well, I can imagine it, but I wouldn't like it.

We are long past being able to say, "No thanks" to computer and internet technology. The only option most of us have is deciding when we are going to learn how to make the best use of this technology. For our children's sake it needs to be now, not later.

See the *Recommended Resources* at the end of this book for further information.

HOMEWORK AND SCHOOLING

Researchers tell us that parental involvement is the most important factor in whether a child does or doesn't do well academically. Too often, though, parents interpret this to mean that they have to stand behind the child's chair, cracking the homework whip.

The danger in this, of course, is that teens start to see their education as something they do for you. When they want to please you, they will work hard at it. But when, as often happens in the teen years, they feel

Up to a certain age you can probably make your child sit in a chair with their science textbook propped open in front of them, but you cannot make them learn.

compelled to separate from you, to establish themselves as separate individuals, they start skipping homework, playing hooky, and failing tests as an expression of this individuality. When this happens, parents press harder and this just makes teens more determined to be their own persons. They try to make that point by doing the opposite of whatever the parents want.

Education is too important to be cannon fodder in a battle of wills between the parent and teen. Academic performance needs to be neutral territory. This shift has to happen in your head first, however.

Influence Not Control

Realize, first of all, that this is an area of influence, not control. Up to a certain age you can probably make your child sit in a chair with their science textbook propped open in front of them, but you cannot make them learn. Only they can engage their brain and make the effort required to do well.

Bribery?

Some parents try bribery. There are a couple problems with this. First of all, it sets a precedent for "buying" behaviour. If a parent will pay $50 for a "B," what will they pay if the teen promises not to smoke or do drugs? And of course, if the teen is already behaving responsibly, but still wants to cash in on this source of money, he or she will have to develop some destructive behaviours just so they can be paid to improve.

> *For Example: Seventeen-year-old Jana works hard in school, earning mostly Bs. She doesn't smoke or do drugs and dates a really nice guy her own age. Her sister, sixteen-year-old Emma, is getting "Ds" and, while she doesn't appear to be doing drugs, her boyfriend is a thirty-year-old with a drinking problem. In desperation, her parents offer Emma $100 per subject if she'll bring her grades up to "Cs" and promise to buy her a car if she'll dump the boyfriend.*

Would anyone be surprised if Jana's grades slip at the next report card and she starts smoking? She's going to have to do something destructive to get her parents to pay her too.

Another problem with bribery is that the ante has to keep going up. The ten-year-old that performed for $20 will need $50 by twelve years of age and $100 by fifteen, and so on. The biggest strike against bribery, however, is that like doing homework for the parent, bribery sets up the wrong motivation.

Motivation from Within

It is *not* the job of parents to tell their teens what to be when they grow up. It *is* the job of parents to help their teens:

- see the future as full of opportunities that those teens can choose from when they are ready;
- understand that the choices they make about their education will limit or enlarge the opportunities they have available to them in the future;
- help them sort through their options and find the direction they want; and
- maximize their potential.

As parents we must accept that we cannot *force* our children to do well in school and we must respect that our teens are rapidly evolving into adults who will make the choices that they decide are best for their own lives. After all, they will have to live with their decisions, and they will have to do the work required to get them where they want to go.

It's all fine and good for a parent to urge their teen to become an astronaut, for example, but there are a million slogging hours of brutally difficult studies (for just one thing) to get through before they're even considered for liftoff. The parent won't be doing that work, the child will.

All the "wanting to please Mom or Dad" in the world isn't going to do them much good when the going gets tough. They must want it for themselves.

The motivation to do well, whatever career choices our teens make, must come from within them. All the "wanting to please Mom or Dad" in the world isn't going to do them much good when the going gets tough. They must want it for themselves. There is, however, much that parents can do to help them.

Give Back Responsibility

Let your teen know that you will help in whatever ways you can, but that what they do with their life will ultimately be up to them. When my teens came home with poor grades and made noises about dropping courses that were important to keeping their educational options open, my response was usually something like this:

"I know you'll decide on what's best for yourself, but if you drop math now, you'll close the door to university, college, and technical schools. You'll be leaving far fewer options for yourself. If you think it would help, we can look into getting a math tutor, but I don't want to push you into something you don't think is best for yourself. After all, this isn't my life we're talking about. When you're in your thirties, earning a minimum-wage living, your father and I will be in our sixties and living out our own lives. We expect to be spending most of our time travelling all over the world. What you do with your own life is really all up to you. You'll be the one living it, not me."

Teens do have dreams, usually very consumeristic, and I have never been above using these dreams to motivate my kids to academic effort!

Articulate Dreams

Most teens would have a hard time identifying what they really want to be when they grow up. Actually, most of us will change careers three or four times in our working lives, so it's not even very useful for a four-teen or fifteen-year-old to pin down exactly what they want to do "for the rest of their lives".

It's even less useful for a parent to define a career path for their teen. As a parent, we would probably lean toward choosing a career for our kids that offers the best opportunities for financial success and security. We would look at a teen who does well in math, for example, and see a future accountant. But trying to convince a fourteen-year-old that spending the rest of their life locked in a room totting up figures and calculating tax advantages would be viewed by them as their worst nightmare come true, a never-ending math class.

But teens do have dreams, usually very consumeristic, and I have never been above using these dreams to motivate my kids to academic effort! You are probably already familiar with many of their dreams (like owning a Porsche), but lead them into conversations that will help them give a little more shape to the future they want for themselves.

> *For Example: Jason may not have any idea what he wants to do for a career, but when he starts to dream out loud, he does know that he wants a hot car, a cabin in the islands, and an apartment in town. He also expects to eat out almost every day, work out at a good gym, and take ski holidays several times a year.*

Articulating dreams like this can lead into conversations about which careers would support this kind of lifestyle. That leads into conversations about which courses and what kinds of grades will be required to qualify for those kinds of careers. See how this works?

It's also very important that consumer-oriented teens truly understand the value of money. See *Chapter Nine* for tips on helping them get

Most kids assume that an $8 per hour salary will buy them everything they want.

real. Until they've had to deal with real budgets and real expenses, most kids assume that an $8 per hour salary will buy them everything they want. And of course they know someone who's doing it! Don't argue with them, just get them busy managing real money for a few months and you won't have to say another word.

While some kids will be motivated by overtly consumeristic dreams, others might be motivated by the flexibility and personal power that some careers offer.

> *For Example: Dana is a mountaineer who dreams about climbing all the big mountains in the world. At sixteen she saves every penny from her part-time job for the expensive gear she needs and even her friends cannot tempt her into throwing money into adolescent money traps like clothes, cds, fast food, and movies. Dana would consider herself the least consumeristic person she knows. However, if her future as a climber plays out the way she dreams it will, she will need lots of money (to support herself, pay for very expensive gear, travel, and participate in costly expeditions) and the career flexibility to take off for weeks and months at a time. She is also more likely to be accepted for major expeditions if she has something extra to offer that would be valuable to the team (eg. medical, physio, photographer, fundraiser, equipment tech, languages, and so on). There are many career choices that would help her realize her dream to be a major league climber. Her parents could help her explore what they might be and find out what training and prerequisites are required.*

"Dreams" are what motivate most of us to try harder. I dream of a future where I'll be able to indulge my passion for travel. That motivates me to invest more in savings and less in lunches out or new clothes. People without dreams are people without hope of a better or more exciting tomorrow. Dreams are very, very powerful. Show your kids how to use their dreams to carry them through endless hours of studying calculus!

Define Options

Keeping educational and career options as wide open as possible is the goal but, in most countries, teens are required, by thirteen or fourteen at least, to start charting a course for themselves. In most schools they choose either an academic or more skill-oriented stream. They must make decisions about taking prerequisites that will give them access to technical schools, the higher level sciences or language requirements demanded by universities, the prerequisite courses and portfolio for art college, or the science courses required for nursing, for example.

As a parent who knows your teen better than anyone else, you can help them sort through an overwhelming variety of possibilities to find some direction. Start by talking about those things that make them happy.

For Example: Sarah spends hours and hours in front of her computer. There isn't anything she doesn't know about accessing the Internet and she's designed a home page for her Mom's business.

Geordie, on the other hand, gets claustrophobia if he has to spend too much time indoors. He spends all his spare time backpacking through the wilderness and at fifteen has already led his Scout troop on numerous trips.

Their biggest advantage will be their own genuine interest.

Those are the places to start. Satisfying and fulfilling jobs are tough to get and keep. Our teens need every advantage they can get and their biggest advantage will be their own genuine interest. They need to be "good" at what they're doing and, usually, that only happens when they are doing something for which they have a passion.

After looking at their passions, talk with them about their personal characteristics. Are they sociable types who prefer working with lots of people around them? Or would they rather kick the door shut and do it themselves? Are they self-motivated and have no trouble getting down to a task on their own? Or are they easily distracted and need more exterior controls?

There are workbooks that are excellent at helping people define career options that would be most compatible for them. *What Colour is my Parachute?* is one I would recommend, but I'm sure there are other good ones too. These kinds of workbooks help bring career paths into focus.

Some of the more diffi-cult or boring things they have to do are just steps on the trail that's going somewhere they want to go.

If teens have some idea where they're going, it helps them see that some of the more difficult or boring things they have to do are just steps on the trail that's going somewhere they want to go. Math 12 may be a difficult slog for Geordie, but if he can see that it's leading toward a career in forestry management, doing which means he'll get to spend the rest of his life tramping around in the woods, then he'll be more motivated to give it the required effort.

When Effort Isn't Enough

When your son or daughter appears to be putting in hours and hours of study time but their marks are chronically poor, there are a few things to look at:

- Do they know how to make notes, summarize chapters, and define the key concepts? Do they have good exam-writing technique? For example: do they go through the exam quickly, answering everything they know the answer for, then return to answering the more difficult questions they aren't sure of? There are books and courses on good exam and study techniques. Ensure that your teen knows how to study effectively.
- Does your teen have good language skills? Do they really understand what they are reading? Can they draw conclusions from what they've read? Can they organize their thoughts into a convincing argument and write that up in the form of an essay? Read their homework to find out. Does it make sense? If it doesn't, look for help in this area because the further they get in school, the more important is their ability to read, understand, and communicate.
- Get involved yourself. One parent I know, whose high school daughter had a learning disability that involved reading, helped her by first of all reading her textbooks out loud to her, then going through and making summarizing notes. The notes gave the daughter a manageable amount of material to study and master. The teen was eager to learn, but the volume of material to be read in the higher grade levels would have meant that the "reading" put up an insurmountable obstacle for her.

She would have ended up in a modified program for kids with learning disabilities, which would have destroyed her motivation. She was capable of mastering the material, she just couldn't read well enough.

- What help is available within the school? Go see the school counsellor yourself and find out. Teens can often take a study block during which an on-duty teacher is available to tutor them in problem areas. Many teachers offer after-school or lunch-hour special-help sessions for students who need a little extra.

- Would a tutor help? Options vary here, from the $4-per-hour student in a senior grade who's "good at math", to the $25-per-hour professional teacher who's moonlighting, to the $350-per-month special learning centres where kids are exposed to all kinds of high-tech testing and computer learning programs.

- Is there any chance your teen has a learning disability? These can be devastating because apparently "smart" kids chronically do poorly in school. Because they are verbally articulate and obviously intelligent, the conclusion is often drawn that they are getting lousy grades because they just aren't trying. This can destroy a teen's motivation. If you think there is any chance of this, push very hard to get your teen tested. If you can't get your school system to do it, pay for it yourself. It's very, very important that your son or daughter be appropriately diagnosed and have a learning program designed for them. They can succeed, but they will need help.

Difficult Teachers

Teachers are no different than the general population. Some are good but others are mediocre or even, bad. At one time or another every kid will run up against a teacher who appears to be a real jerk. As a parent, the temptation is to jump in and get your kid transferred out of that teacher's class, but think very hard about this:

It's possible that this teacher sees genuine ability in your teen and, while their methods may be crude, what they are doing is pushing so hard that your teen is getting uncomfortable. Your teen is being challenged to do their best and they may not be used to doing that in an academic context.

Throughout life your teen will run up against people with whom they have personality conflicts or who just don't appear to like them.

> *If your teen can handle this situation and get out of it what they need, they will emerge empowered.*

They need practice dealing with these kinds of people and situations. Rescue them from dealing with this situation and they will have to learn how to deal with it somewhere down the road when the stakes may be much higher and you won't be able to rescue them.

If your teen can handle this situation and get out of it what they need – grades that reflect their effort and ability – they will emerge empowered. We all need these kinds of triumphs in our emotional kit bags.

Lighten Up

Yes, it's important that your teens do well in school and, yes, it's a good idea to get the right prerequisite courses lined up so they can apply for the post-secondary education they want. But it's not the end of the world if they don't. Some kids just can't summon up the motivation and just can't get any kind of handle on what they want to do. For them, it may be best to work for a year or two. Minimum wage can be sobering and more than a few kids have been motivated by that reality.

Remember that it's not your life, it's theirs and they'll have to figure it out for themselves. Course work can always be "made up" in adult-education programs and prerequisites can be picked up in community colleges. Yes, it may take them longer to finish up, but when they finally know what they want, they'll go after it with a passion that will make their goal achievable for them.

~ Chapter Nine ~

MANAGING MONEY

We're All Self Taught

Money management is one of the most important life skills a parent could teach their children. Fortunately, it's also one of the easiest skills to teach. What it boils down to is:

1. Ensure they have money.
2. Stand back.
3. Watch them learn.

THEIR OWN MONEY

From even a very young age, children need to be managing their own money. I remember that when my oldest son was about four, he got into the habit of harassing me for "stuff", particularly at check-out counters. When this became really annoying I realized it was time for him to learn something about managing money. So we started giving him an allowance, which we paid out in nickels. Of course he thought he had a fortune. The next time we went to the store I warned him that if he was going to want to buy something, he should bring his bag of money along. Sure enough, we got to the check-out counter and they were selling pens with big Santa Claus heads on them. He figured he should have one of these. "No problem," said I. "You have your bag of nickels, let's count out how many you'll need."

He had forty nickels and the Santa Claus pen was going to cost him thirty of them, which shocked him. I cheerfully told him that he could

> *Teens must have money*
> *before they can learn to*
> *manage money.*

buy the pen if he wanted, but reminded him to think about what else he might want to spend money on this week.

I've used the example of a young child here, but the principle for teens is no different. Whether they are getting an allowance from you or pumping gas at the corner station, they must *have* money before they can learn to manage money.

Saving

After my young son had a few months of this hands-on money management he noticed that some things would always be out of his reach to buy because their purchase price was far more than his weekly allowance. At this time I introduced the concept of saving. In fact, once our kids got a little older we actually mandated that they must save a certain proportion of their allowance and earnings toward a major goal of their own choosing (either a "thing" or a monetary figure). We did this because we noticed that our children just couldn't seem to think really long term. The idea that they could actually save a large amount of money - enough for a video-game system or a bike – was simply incomprehensible to them. We had to prove to them that this could be done. I well remember the first time my youngest son's bank account reached the magic number of $100. It was like he had won the lottery. He really hadn't believed he could do it and he hung onto that $100 for a very long time.

Millions of people, crushed under huge burdens of consumer debt, were never taught that they could save the money for a couch or a car or a vacation. They assume that the only way to get these things is to put them on credit and pay for them later (with interest). Honestly, it just never occurs to them that they could save for things. They've never seen anyone do it and they just don't understand the process. Say "no" to the ice cream truck today so that you can have a new bike tomorrow. No one ever taught them this.

Once your teen has reached their savings goal, don't interfere in their decision about how to spend it. You may think spending $75 on a front row seat to a rock concert is a waste of money, but all the talking in the world is not going to convince your teen of that. They need to spend their savings, go to the concert, and come to the realization themselves that a two-hour concert is not a reasonable exchange for three months of saving. Then again, you might be wrong. We all have different values and when "The Three Tenors" came to my town one New Year's Eve, lots of mature-minded adults spent thousands of dollars for a (less than two-hour) concert. Some of them came away from the concert realizing that they'd wasted their money, but others we're thrilled with their evening and said they'd do it again anytime.

The point is that teens only develop their own values around money and learn to make relatively wise money management decisions if they truly make their own decisions. Those decisions may not be the same ones that the parent would make, but we need to respect their decisions as being right for them.

They only learn to make wise money management decisions if they truly make their own decisions.

Making Mistakes

The way most of us learn not to do something is by making mistakes and living with the consequences

It can be very hard for you to stand by while your teens make some unwise spending choices, but it is the best way for them to learn to become savvy consumers. Like most parents, I went through a period when my young teens insisted that their boots had to be $140 Doc Martins and their jeans had to have $85 designer labels. We argued endlessly about this stuff.

I solved the problem by deciding what I could afford to spend for new school clothes, then giving them the money to spend as they saw fit. Every August, before the new school year started, I would give them a specified amount of money for new clothes and they would manage it themselves. Often they augmented this clothing allowance with their own earnings so they could buy their Doc Martins, but sometimes it meant that they made a choice to go with no-name brands. Managing their clothing allowance themselves made them highly critical of workmanship, experts on fabric labels, and avid "sales" shoppers. It also brought peace to our home again.

Teens will make money management mistakes (not unlike adults), but better they should learn from $50 mistakes as teens than $50,000 mistakes as adults.

THE CHORES AND ALLOWANCE DEBATE

Should teens get an allowance just because they're breathing or should it be in exchange for chores performed? This question can be debated from two points of view.

1. Family Income Belongs to Everyone

Family income belongs to "the family" and every member should receive a share of it for their own use. Thus, a teen would receive an allowance, regardless of whether or not they do chores. This "share" is not payment for services, but a right by membership. Chores are done, not for payment, but because everyone shares the family responsibilities.

Teens brains are loaded with a software program that screens out pictures of dirty dishes, laundry, and grimy bathtubs.

Pros: A warm fuzzy feeling because this is an egalitarian-type plan that appeals to those of us who came of age in the 60s. Every member shares the income and every member of the family shares the responsibilities. It sounds really good.

Cons: It sounds too good! Teens don't like doing chores and their brains are loaded with a software program that actually screens out pictures of dirty dishes, laundry, and grimy bathtubs from their visual field. So they don't even see these things. Most kids need an incentive to do chores and money motivates them.

2. Money for Chores

The opposite point of view states that the parents worked for the money, no one gets paid for doing nothing (an arguable point!) and teens shouldn't get paid for doing nothing. In these households the teens have a list of chores and, when they are done, they get paid.

Pros: Money is a motivator so chores are more likely to get done (although children who can't even read yet become savvy negotiators, mortgaging "future services" for money in hand today).

Cons: This approach is a bit cold-blooded and business-like for some of us. Also, the system falls apart once the kids acquire some outside income (eg. paper route). Once they start earning big money, they won't be willing to do a whole list of chores for a measly $10 per week. They'll tell you to forget the allowance, they don't want to do chores anymore. So if "chores for money" has been the strategy, the parent is up a creek without a paddle.

What to do?

Every parent has to find the path that is the best match with their own values and their own kids, but I believe that the answer lies somewhere in the philosophical middle. In family council meetings, talk about the need for "the family" to do the work of the family. Develop a family culture that sees household responsibilities as a family responsibility. As a parent, respect the decisions that the family makes about "good enough for us" standards and don't expect kids to take on duties that have already been negotiated out of the family standards package.

At the same time, however, talk about access to family income and how unfair it would be for a member who is chronically failing to meet their responsibilities, to also be receiving the same benefits (including allowance, money for sports, clothes, and so on). While it's awkward to make a direct tie-in between cleaning the bathroom and paying for ski lessons, family members who are not fulfilling the responsibilities they've agreed to need to experience consequences. Even young children will understand this. In fact, the younger a child is, the more rigid their stand on this topic will probably be. Youngsters have a keen sense of justice and fair play. So don't think that your family is too young to work this out.

Bring the chores and allowance issue to a family council meeting and work it out as a family.

Talk about the need for "the family" to do the work of the family.

PART TIME JOBS

Teens who work up to fourteen hours per week at a part-time job apparently do better in school. This makes sense to me. I know that once my own kids had part-time jobs they became much better students. I think this happened for two good reasons. First of all, they became much better at organizing their time. They started doing homework and studying before the last minute because the "night before" the exam or the project was due, they could be at work. Similarly, they did their household chores ahead of time too, because on their night off they wanted to be out with friends, not cleaning the bathtub. Part-time jobs made them efficient time managers.

As a parent, watching them make mistakes with their money is a lot easier to take, knowing it really is their own money!

Second, I think they became better students because they realized, after a while, how hard they had to work for their minimum wage. Pumping gas or flipping burgers or loading trucks is hard work, often under stressful conditions. They would look at me, plinking away at a keyboard all day (how hard could that be - and she sits too!) for several times their salary and they'd say to themselves, "Gotta get me an education." A part-time job is very motivating.

I also believe in part-time jobs for teens because it gives them the autonomy they crave. They make their own money and they manage their own money. As a parent, watching them make mistakes with their money is a lot easier to take, knowing it really is their own money! You can still sit down with them and work out a money management plan, but the money really is theirs and the level of pride in themselves will be high. It will give them such a sense of capability. Because they know that they can earn money for themselves, and take care of themselves, their faith in themselves soars.

Money Management Plans

Once your teens start earning money, sit them down and help them draw up a money-management plan. This doesn't mean that they aren't managing their own money – far from it! A money-management plan puts the planner in the driver's seat and will help teens form a life-long habit of planning their financial affairs. Think of those millions of people being crushed by their consumer debt because they don't have money-management skills. Your job as a parent is to teach these skills. Remember though, that as parent you are just their guide in the process, not the decision maker. This is *their* money-management plan.

A typical plan might look something like this:

Long-term savings for car	25%
Long-term savings for college tuition	25%
Short-term savings (holidays, leather jacket, skiis, etc.)	25%
Everyday spending (food, movies, clothes, gifts, etc.)	25%
TOTAL:	100%

In what proportions or for what goals they divide up their money is much, much less important than that they create the plan. Suggest that they live with their plan for six months, then evaluate how well it is working for them and make any changes they think would make it work better for them. Help them evaluate all their banking options – from the sock drawer to credit unions to traditional big-name banks. If they have long-term savings goals, help them investigate different savings/investment plans: savings accounts, GICs, term deposits, or mutual funds. It's never too young to start a retirement savings plan either, because they can have significant tax advantage. Don't you wish you'd put $50 per month away from age fifteen?

Since they work hard for their money, they should see their money work hard for them.

Promote the idea that since they work hard for their money, they should see their money work hard for them.

She'd almost missed an opportunity to give her son an important life-skill – buying a car!

ROLE MODELLING

Like every other aspect of raising children, the behaviour we parents model will have more effect on them than anything we say. We model good money management skills or we don't, and each experience is a learning opportunity. If you've made mistakes that you are trying to correct, explain that. Show them how much carrying those credit card balances has cost you. Discuss the decision you made to buy the cheaper lawn mover that is too underpowered for your property. Be proud of the great decision you made to buy your home in an area that has now increased in value and explain what things need to be taken into account when making decisions about real estate. Give your teens tools for going into the world and making good money-management decisions.

> *For Example: One mother recounted how on the day that she had decided to buy a car she had been looking at for several days, her fourteen-year-old son asked to come along. She wondered why. He just shrugged. So he came and observed the negotiations going back and forth between the salesperson and his mom. Driving away after the sale was completed, he bubbled with excitement and pride in his mom. This had been his first glimpse of the hard-nosed business woman that, of course, he'd never seen before. She was just his mom. Furthermore, the experience had taught him how to buy a car. He'd had a front-row seat on the deal-making and, as he said, he wouldn't have had any idea how to get the best deal if he hadn't seen his mom in action. She realized that she'd almost missed an opportunity to give her son an important life-skill – buying a car!*

In everything you do, talk to your kids and answer their questions. Explain why you're investing in registered retirement funds that give you a tax break instead of just stashing money in a savings account that pays 4% interest and offers no tax advantages. Tell them why you're driving a ten-year-old car instead of a new one. If you're going to buy a new fridge, ask them to help you price it out and weigh the benefits of the different models (and decide for themselves why the family won't be purchasing the $1800 model that does everything but make beds).

Teens and young adults are often loathe to do what their parents tell them to do, but do not mistake that for lack of influence. By showing

Seeing the big picture
... is what maturing is all about.

them, on a daily basis, the effects (both positive and negative) of your own money-management decisions, you are supplying them with invaluable information with which to make their own decisions.

The Family Money

Ask your son or daughter to help you manage the family money for three to six months. This experience will be an important financial eye opener for them.

Sit down together at the end of the month and have your teen pay all the family bills (by cheque, computer, or telephone). Then have them spreadsheet all the family expenses. If you're not already doing this, it's a great way to see where the family money is or isn't going.

Just take a large sheet of paper and make columns, heading them with titles like: income, spending money, food, utilities, vehicle expenses, mortgage, entertainment, clothing, and so on. Then gather up all your receipts for the month (plus credit card bills, ATM withdrawals, and cheque-book entries) and have your teen enter the figures under the appropriate columns. Over several months, this kind of "spread sheeting" will give you and your teen a good picture of what it costs the family to live in its current style.

Talk about the family's money-management plan and what might be done differently. Does the family really need two phone lines? Where will the money for a holiday come from? What will need to be sacrificed to get another vehicle?

Simply by virtue of where they are in their development as human beings, adolescents are very self-centred. Having them participate in the family's money management is a golden opportunity to help them grow up a little more. When they can see, in very real terms, that their personal requests must be juggled with all the other needs of the family (including retirement savings for their parents), it gives them a greater sense of responsibility for themselves. They are more likely, then, to make "saving for college" part of their personal money-management plan, for example, instead of just assuming that Mom or Dad will cover this. They start to see the bigger picture and that's what maturing is really all about.

Money-Management Grad School – The Credit Card

Sooner or later, everyone gets a credit card. The credit companies make sure of that – inundating us with unsolicited cards and assurances that we're a Pre-Approved, Recommended Client! It's heady stuff for newly-graduated kids and concrete proof that they're now adults.

After they've "graduated", so to speak, from Money-Management 101 (stick to their own money-management plan, spreadsheet family finances, and so on), think about preparing your teen for the shark-infested waters of credit by giving them a credit card to use while you can still keep an eye on them.

In our own home we did this because our eldest son was doing a lot of travelling and we were concerned that he have a safety net in case of car trouble or unexpected major expenses while he was away from home. We took a credit card that we didn't use ourselves, had the financial limit fixed at $2,000, and had a card issued in his name. It worked very well and after a while I realized what a great tool this was for teaching him how to handle credit. After he'd had it for a few months he started to use it for gas and other expenses. Since the account was in my name, the bill still came to me and I could see that he wasn't getting carried away. Like all of us, he had months where he spent more than he'd thought he did and was shocked at the bottom line. He learned to keep his receipts and run a balance for himself. He learned self-discipline and how to handle credit – lessons he'd begun many years before when he decided that a pen wasn't worth an extra twenty nickels just because it had a plastic Santa Claus head glued on top!

You can teach money-management skills but most parents don't have much luck teaching their kids much about the value of money.

A FINAL WORD: The Value of Money

You can teach money-management skills but most parents won't have much luck teaching their kids too much about the value of money. Don't despair. Life will teach that lesson.

What I mean, is that in most of our households, there is milk in the fridge, heat pours magically out of floor registers, and money for anything genuinely important always turns up. By and large, the money that our teens make gets spent on things that they want much more than they need.

For Example:

They want another pair of jeans – they won't go naked without them.

They want to go out for a burger – they won't starve if they don't get it.

They want concert tickets – they don't have to choose between the tickets and the rent.

They want to go to the Grad Dance – they won't have the heat turned off if they go.

In our homes, we already provide everything they *need*. Most kids spend 100% of their incomes on things they *want*. Choosing between wants and needs is not something they usually have to do until they leave home. I only mention this because, so often, parents despair about the things their teens spend money on. "Two thousand dollars for a mountain bike!" shrieks one father. "I didn't spend two thousand dollars on my first car! When is that kid going to learn the value of money?"

He will learn the value of money when he has to choose between bikes and rent, or between food and concert tickets. Real life will teach its own money-management lessons soon enough. So relax, you're off the hook on this one.

Chapter Ten

KEEPING THEM SAFE

Parents today are scared, and we should be. Our teens cope with more danger on a daily basis than we ever did. Knowing that, also understand that their own instincts about danger are the most important defence our teens have. Overprotection is the most dangerous thing we can do to our teens. There are two reasons for this:

- it stifles their own instinct for self-protection;
- it encourages the rebellion factor.

Nurturing Their Instinct for Self-Protection

We cannot walk beside our teens every moment of the day, making on-the-spot decisions about what is safe or unsafe. Their own instincts are the only real protection they have out there. If you have been so busy making and enforcing rules to protect your teen that they think their safety is your job, they'll likely leave it up to you and not use their own brain or listen to their own instincts.

For Example: Alec's parents have given him a long list of what he may and may not do. He may ride the subway until seven in the evening, but after that he has to call them for a ride. Alec assumes this means the subway is safe until seven and he's very comfortable using it. So comfortable, that he doesn't pay any attention to the other passengers in the cars he gets into or where he sits. He is shocked, one afternoon, to be backed into a corner by a gang of thugs who relieve him of money, watch, and jacket – at knife point. After all, it was only three in the afternoon. The subway should be

We must help them develop their own judgment and encourage their own instincts for self-protection. It is the only way to keep them really safe.

safe at that time, his parents said so. But that afternoon, his head buried in a comic book, he'd paid no attention to the fact that the car he entered had no one but this gang of troublemakers in it. His instinct for self-protection had been stifled by the list of rules that his parents had designed to keep him safe. He wasn't thinking for himself.

Parents cannot accompany their teens everywhere. We must help them develop their own judgment and encourage their own instincts for self-protection. It is the only way to keep them really safe.

The Rebellion Factor

Another reason for avoiding the "rules to keep them safe" route is what I call the rebellion factor. Specific rules that tell a child where they can and cannot go and what they can and cannot do, may work reasonably well up until the teen hits puberty; then watch out. A parent's need to control runs head-on into a teen's need for autonomy and the parent will always lose. If nothing else, time is on the teen's side. No matter how much effort we as a parent might try to put into "controlling" our teen, they are getting older every day. They will become an adult. They will move out. They will take control of their own life. That, in fact, is what we are aiming for.

A rebellious teen isn't making decisions based on what they think is best for themselves, they're simply reacting mindlessly against whatever their parent's rules are. This is really, really dangerous.

Teens who've been brought up with a list of rigid, controlling rules tend to rebel once the hormonal tsunami hits. And, unfortunately, rebellion doesn't usually involve the brain. A rebellious teen isn't making decisions based on what they think is best for themselves, they're simply reacting mindlessly against whatever their parent's rules are. This is really, really dangerous.

Every family member needs to operate within a set of guidelines that are flexible and respectful of the degree of personal responsibility each member is developing.

Developing Personal Responsibility

Some parents say that they'll give their teen more freedom once they show some responsibility, but it doesn't work that way. Responsibility is not something that arrives like a gift on a pre-defined birthday. "Responsibility" is really the ability to foresee both the short and long-term consequences of a behaviour and to make a decision that takes those consequences into account.

Teens develop responsibility when they have acquired experience in dealing with the consequences of their behaviour or decisions. It is impossible for a teen to develop responsibility or demonstrate responsibility unless they have the opportunity to acquire that experience through situations in which they make their own decisions and then deal with the consequences of those decisions.

For Example: Every morning Lisa's mom hands her two transit tickets – one to get to school, one to get home. She doesn't give Lisa the whole book because she's sure Lisa will lose it. She doesn't just leave the book of tickets on the fridge for Lisa to help herself because she's sure Lisa will forget to take the tickets. There is no reason in the world for Lisa to remember her own transit tickets; her mother is already working overtime doing her thinking for her.

If Lisa's mom decided, instead, to teach Lisa to take responsibility for herself, she could start by putting the book of transit tickets on the fridge, then advise Lisa to help herself each morning. If Lisa forgets, she will have to deal with the problem herself – walk the five miles home, borrow some money from friends, or wait at school for three hours until her mom gets off work and can pick her up.

Once Lisa is remembering to take the transit tickets, her mom could take the next step and give her the book to keep in her room. If Lisa loses it, she will be responsible for replacing it. The final step in nur-

turing Lisa's responsibility for taking care of herself would be to have her purchase her own transit tickets each month, leaving Mom out of it altogether.

Remembering to take transit tickets may seem like a long way from making decisions about personal safety, but they both require teens to take personal responsibility for themselves, not rely on parents to do their thinking for them. Teens need lots and lots of practice making decisions. They also need opportunities to make mistakes, so they learn that they do, indeed, have to thoroughly think things through. Lisa probably will forget her transit tickets a few times and she'll probably hate having to walk home or ask others for bus fare. She'll really hate having to cool her heels at school for three hours waiting for her parent to get off work and pick her up. But it won't kill her and she will really understand it finally – she has to think things through in the morning. If she's the forgetful type, her mom or dad could help her by brainstorming some strategies for how she'll remember her transit tickets. For example, Lisa could make a checklist, tape a note to the mirror, or pack her bag the night before. But Lisa's parents won't be helping her develop personal responsibility if they continue to stand at the door, tickets in hand, doing her thinking for her.

MANAGING OUR OWN FEAR

Teens often interpret our fear as a lack of faith in themselves. We need to be explicit about what we are actually afraid of.

For Example: Carol calls her mom from a new friend's house. She wants to spend the night. Her mother has never met this friend and knows nothing about the family or the home. She doesn't even know where it is. She tells Carol that "...this just isn't a good idea." When Carol pushes her harder, she says, "I'm just not comfortable with this."

Carol, by now very upset, says "You never trust me! You think I'm going to have boys over and do drugs and who knows what. You never trust me!"

In fact, her mother doesn't think Carol is going to do any of that. However, not knowing anything about the home, she actually fears things like Carol being exposed to drunkenness, drug use, and abu-

> *Teens usually think that our decisions are based on what we believe they will do. In fact, our decisions about safety are usually based on what we fear others will do.*

sive behaviour. She fears the terrors of the unknown - Carol could be raped and murdered there.

If we can be open and honest about what our fears are actually about, our teens can sometimes alleviate them. They often have information about other families that they might consider irrelevant but that parents might find helpful.

For Example: Hearing that their daughter's friend lives next door to someone the parents know well, might help alleviate concern.

Because of where they are in their development, teens are very self-centred. They will usually think that our decisions are based on what we think they will do. In fact, our decisions about safety are usually based on what we fear others will do, so be explicit about your fears and concerns.

For Example: One young teen was furious because his dad wouldn't let him take public transit after nine in the evening. They fought endlessly about this, with the teen exclaiming that, "I'm fifteen, I'm nearly a man! Why do you always have to treat me like a baby?" What the father finally realized was that his objection had nothing to do with his son's age. It had to do with the fact that after nine in the evening, anyone catching a bus to their house from the nearest subway stop would have to wait an hour between buses, in a very dark and unsafe spot. The father himself would not have been com- fortable at that spot and the issue had nothing to do with age. When he was able to explain this to his son, and the teen came to under- stand that he was not being treated like a baby, they were able to make some compromises with which they both could both live.

We must also understand and accept that each step our child takes away from us will be uncomfortable, at the least. Sometimes it will be downright painful.

For Example: I often think that if I hadn't broken my ankle when my eldest son was in grade three, I would still be walking him all the way to school. I was certainly prepared to. Every step away that my kids took was painful – first day at daycare, first week at school, first sleep-over Cub camp, first no-adults backpacking trip, first time they drove "downtown" by themselves, first time my eldest drove himself through the snow-covered Rockies in the winter. I survived all these traumas and I'll survive those yet to come.

There's no doubt it's a fine line between trusting your instincts for danger and accepting the discomfort that each new freedom brings. Determining which side an activity falls on can sometimes be difficult, but it is often helpful to ask yourself why you are saying "No" to something. Is it because you can identify a real danger in the activity, or is it because you don't want to deal with the discomfort?

PARENTING IN A DANGEROUS WORLD

Current thinking in parent education holds that there are three basic styles of parenting.

Autocratic Parents

...are into absolute control. The parent is the authoritarian figure and maintains control by reward and punishment. The teens of these parents are either rebels or broken spirits. In neither case are they learning how to make good and responsible decisions for themselves because they are not allowed to. The "broken spirit" does whatever she is told because she has given up thinking for herself. The "rebel" does the exact opposite of whatever his parents want, so is not thinking for himself either. These teens have no freedom, only boundaries that attempt to confine and stifle them from thinking for themselves.

Permissive Parents

...believe teens should be allowed to do their own thing. Anything the teen wants is just fine. This style of parenting creates very insecure teens because, from their point of view, no one cares about them, and no one cares enough to set limits on their behaviour. These teens experience unlimited freedom with no boundaries.

Participatory Parents

...encourage teens to express their point of view. While the teens may not always get what they want, they always get a fair hearing. Their parents set guidelines that are sensitive to the teens' growing need to make decisions for themselves. They encourage personal responsibility and give the teens lots of opportunities to practise decision making. Their teens experience freedom within limits that adjust appropriately to the circumstances and the teens growing maturity.

Negotiate Expanding Limits

Teaching teens how to make responsible decisions about their own safety involves providing freedom within expanding limits. Talk to your teen about the freedom they want. Together, make a list of freedom goals:

For Example:
- *to go downtown to the movies*
- *to use the car to take her friends to the beach*
- *to go backpacking without adults*

As a parent, really examine these freedom goals and define what it is about these goals that concerns you.

For Example:
- *You have no problem with your teen going downtown to the movies, it's the coming home late at night on public transit that is the concern. In fact, it's not the public transit itself, but the fact that after he gets off the subway, he will have to wait at a dark and lonely bus stop up to an hour between buses after nine at night.*
- *You have faith in your teen's driving ability, but the beach is over an hour's drive away and she'll have to navigate some serious freeways to get there. You're afraid that she'll get lost and end up in the*

*You're concerned that her friends will be so
rambunctious in the car that they'll distract her.*

*wrong end of town, or worse. You're also concerned that her friends
will be so rambunctious in the car that they'll distract her.*
*• You know your son is a veteran of many, many backpacking trips
and, in fact, has been credited with getting other adults out of trouble, but he's only fourteen!*

Together, brainstorm ways your teens can accomplish these goals in
steps that you can live with.

For example:
*• When your son and his friends come go to the movies and head
home, they could call you or another parent to pick them up at the*

Work through "what if" scenarios with your teen. Your teen's resourcefulness and street smarts will probably surprise and reassure you. They're not stupid.

final subway stop. Another alternative, if the kids are really feeling the need to express their independence, would be for them to all chip in on a cab ride home.

• *When you talk to your daughter you discover that it's only her best friend who will be driving to the beach with her. To give them more experience with freeway driving, you could take a trial run with them one afternoon, your daughter driving and her friend navigating, while you sit in the back seat. Satisfy yourself that they know how to read freeway signs and what to do if they take the wrong exit.*

• *Agree on a schedule of backpacking trips, with the first "no-adults" trip being a route that is relatively easy to navigate, has lots of other backpacker traffic, and is only a couple days long. The next trip could be longer or to a more remote location.*

As a parent, be specific about your fears. Pull apart situations that make you uneasy and look for ways to address those concerns. Does your backpacking son have all the survival skills and the gear he needs? Could you give your daughter more freeway-driving experience? Would having your son or daughter take a personal safety course be helpful? (You could take it with them.) Are you being overly cautious about the transit stop?

Work through "what if" scenarios with your teen.

For Example: What if the bus doesn't come and while you're waiting somebody tries to pick you up? What if they take the wrong freeway exit? What if one of the backpackers falls and breaks their leg?

Your teen's resourcefulness and street smarts will probably surprise and reassure you. They're not stupid.

CURFEWS and CHECK-INS

As a family, take a new perspective on curfews, the pre-set time at which someone must be home. Think about switching to "check-in times", a time at which someone must either be home or call in.

The purpose of a curfew or check-in time for any member of the family is to alert others that they may need help if they don't make contact after a certain time. In that sense, all members of the family have informal check-in times when they're expected back from work, school, or social activities. It is helpful if the teen can come to understand that check-in times are necessary for the whole family and that he or she isn't being treated like a baby.

> *For Example: If Mom is expected home from her night school class at ten o'clock, no one worries about her at nine. But if she's not home by eleven, and she hasn't called to say she'll be delayed, something may be very wrong. She may need help.*

If there is no set time at which a teen is expected home, then there is no time at which the alarm bells go off, warning other family members that the teen may need help. Since that puts the teen (or any other family member) "out there" on their own, it's not something most parents are comfortable with. As a family, discuss check-in times for each of you – times when you'll either be home or will call to say when you'll be home.

> *For Example: On work days, Dad agrees that he'll be home by six o'clock or call. Tod, who's in grade five, agrees that on school days he'll be home by twenty minutes after three, or will call. Jessie at age sixteen, agrees that on nights when she's working at her part-time job, she'll be home forty-five minutes after her shift ends, or she'll call.*

Ask teens what time they think it would be reasonable for them to be home on a weeknight or weekend. Curfews don't need to be inscribed in stone; they should adjust as events require. As a parent, be open to the realities of your teen's life. What time does the movie actually let out? How long does it really take to eat a pizza? Negotiate times you can both live with.

"Check-ins" are much like curfews, except that at the pre-set time the teen calls home rather than actually comes home. At that time they can report where they are, that they're safe, and negotiate a return home time according to what they are doing and how they plan to get home. Check-in times often make more sense than curfews because they are less rigid and more in sync with a democratic style of family life. As teens grow older and take on more and more autonomy, check-ins also make the transition to an adult-to-adult relationship (because we all need to use them) better than curfews, which will be unacceptable to an older teen or young adult.

As parents we also need to respect the check-in times we've agreed to.

For Example: Leave a note on the fridge saying where you are. "Gone to the movies – back about eleven. Love Mom and Dad." If your plans change and you decide to stay out longer, it's only respect- ful of other family members that you call and (leave a message on the machine if no one is home) giving a new "be home by" time.

After all, kids worry about their parents too.

THRILLS AND CHILLS

Some teens have an overwhelming need to test themselves, and parents have an overwhelming need to protect them. However, the more parents try to stifle a teen's search for thrills, the more likely the teen will find them some way. On their own, teens are more likely to get hurt.

Suggest exciting alternatives to risky activities. Those teens who hunger for an adrenaline rush could be interested in mountain biking, whitewater rafting, rock climbing, parachuting, snowboarding, alpine skiing, or windsurfing. Many community centres offer reasonably priced adventure opportunities for teens. Or help your teen find a part-time job to finance his recreation. These kinds of adrenaline-based adventures are so appealing to kids that many rehabilitation programs for teens in trou- ble are based on them. If your teen is a kid who needs this kind of chal- lenge, help him or her find ways to safely work it out.

Other teens need to test themselves physically. Suggest that they run, cycle, backpack, weight train, climb mountains, or join a track club. Look for situations that satisfy their need for challenge with qualified instruc- tion and coaching.

Some teens are hungry for new experiences and want to see the

*Too often the kids that we think would be a good influence
on our teens, may not be.*

world. Before they take off on their own, investigate student exchange programs and work programs in developing countries. Look for ways that they can satisfy their need for adventure in an environment that offers some support.

Work with your teen to find reasonable alternatives to risky behaviour.

> *Work with your teen to find reasonable*
> *alternatives to risky behaviour.*

FRIENDS

We used to assume that "peer pressure" automatically meant trouble. In fact, most peer pressure is probably positive. Teens bolster each other's self esteem, prop up each other's egos, commiserate over problems, and encourage each other. They help each other, not just in terms of psychological support, but in tangible things like borrowing money, getting jobs, sharing clothes, doing school work, and helping with chores.

They are each other's best friends and at no time in life is that network more supportive or important than during adolescence. They give each other a sense of belonging that is so important to teens' emotional well-being.

It's a good idea not to be too quick to judge your teen's friends. Too often the kids that we, as adults, think would be a good influence on our teens, may not be. They may just be really, really good at impressing adults. The teen who looks like a rebel may be the one with enough backbone to help your teen out of a jam. After all, it takes guts to get your tongue pierced!

> *Most peer pressure is probably positive. They are each other's best friends and at no time in life is that network more supportive or important than during adolescence.*

Without being obtrusive, look for ways to get to know your teen's friends. Offer to give them rides, take them camping with you, and accept them into your home. Many parents have found that giving their teens a rec room that is a "kids only zone" or purchasing something like a pool table, are worthwhile investments in keeping their teens and their friends at home.

When Peer Pressure Isn't Positive

Approach negative peer pressure with your teens from the angle that they, rather than their friends know what is best for themselves. They are smart and should be making the decisions that are best for themselves.

Make it clear, "Everyone was doing it," will never be an acceptable reason for their behaviour. You expect them to make their own decisions. Only wimps and wusses let other kids make their decisions for them.

Make it clear, "Everyone was doing it," will never be an acceptable reason for their behaviour.

They should be in control of themselves, not being controlled by someone else who isn't half as smart as them.

Refusal Strategies

Encourage your teens to follow these steps when their instincts are whispering little warning messages to them:

1. Observe the Situation
Look and listen. What's going on? What is likely to go down? What are their instincts telling them is likely to happen?

2. Evaluate the Pros and Cons
What's in it for them? What are the risks? What are short and long term consequences of being part of this?

3. Make a Decision
Clearly decide what to do, because indecision leaves us vulnerable to teasing.

4. Act
Depending on the situation, this could be to:
- Refuse – "Don't feel like it." "No way." "Can't" "That's dumb."
- Make an excuse – "I'd be grounded for ten years." "I'll barf my guts out." "I have to get up in the morning." "I'm allergic to that."
- Come up with a better idea – "Nah, that doesn't sound like much fun, why don't we ...instead?"
- Leave – Either quietly, or by making an excuse or a joke out of it – "You guys are all crazy!"

BE AVAILABLE

Let your kids know that you are available to pick them up, anyplace and anytime they feel they need a way out. Also make a pact that if and when they call for that ride, you won't harangue, lecture, or interrogate them at that time. This gives

Give them the support to venture out... and an escape hatch to leave.

them an "emergency escape hatch" that they can count on. From your point of view, it gives you the assurance that if your teen is in trouble he will call you.

> *For Example: When my youngest son was about 15, the kids in his school took to booking hotel rooms to hold all-night parties. These were nice hotels and I couldn't imagine why they'd accept a booking from teens in the mood to party, but they did. For the first couple weekends we said a flat, "No". But we soon realized that by forbidding these hotel parties they were acquiring an overwhelming desirability that might push our son to choose to disobey us. After all, he was permitted to stay overnight at friend's homes on the weekends and it would have been easy for him to arrange such a sleepover that actually took him to one of these parties. We worried that attending under those conditions would not offer him any escape plan if he needed it.*
>
> *After much discussion with him about how we trusted his judgment and how we knew that he would do what was best for him, we agreed that he could attend a hotel party the next Saturday night. The stipulation was that if, for any reason, he was uncomfortable, he would call us at any hour of the night and we would be there, no questions asked.*
>
> *At eight o'clock Saturday night I dropped him off at the hotel, only slightly comforted by the fact that it was very nice hotel at which I'd attended many meetings. At half past eleven the phone rang. Could we pick him up? When I did, he mumbled something about the party being boring and that was that. Whether the party was boring or whether there was something going on he chose not to be part of, I'll probably never know. But as parents we gave him the support he needed to venture out a bit, as well as the escape hatch to leave.*

Letting Go Is Hard To Do

Knowing that "control" is just an illusion, where teens are concerned, is not really helpful in terms of calming a parent's fears about their teens safety. It is a scary world out there. Hopefully, however, this chapter has given you some ideas for supporting your teens and ensuring that they have the skills they need to protect themselves.

~ Chapter Eleven ~

DISCIPLINE THAT TEACHES

Parents want to know, "What will make my teens do what I want them to do?" If you've read this far, though, you already know that controlling your teens is a fantasy. You might think you're doing it, but teens will always find ways to do what they really want to do.

What is Discipline Then?

In the movies, and in some segments of society, desperate parents sent their misbehaving sons to military school to "acquire some discipline". The idea of learning discipline is a good one, but military schools don't usually teach it, they impose it. Getting up at five in the morn-

> *Where punishment is focused on the past, discipline is future-oriented and educational.*

ing to do five thousand push-ups isn't about discipline, it's about getting whipped if you don't. I wonder how many privates on leave get up at five in the morning to do five thousand push-ups?

If "discipline" isn't making someone do what's good for them, what is it? Discipline is education for life. It provides guidelines for making good decisions. Where punishment is focused on the past, discipline is future-oriented and educational. It teaches teens how to make decisions for themselves that are positive and appropriate to whatever situation they find themselves in.

Won't Punishment Work?

The purpose of punishment is to make teens obedient to parents. That might sound good at first, but think about it for a moment. Every day your teens get a little older and, during adolescence, the march toward independence becomes a windsprint. You won't be there to make all your teens' decisions for them. Is "obedience" really the way to go? Wouldn't you rather be teaching them how to make good and appropriate decisions for themselves, even when you don't agree with them? Punishment doesn't teach anything about decision making.

> *For Example: Jenny came home drunk. With alcoholism in their family history, her parents are worried sick about Jenny so they punish her by grounding her for a month.*

Punishment establishes a battleground for power. Teens learn that if they are caught they will be punished. The objective becomes "not getting caught".

Jenny hasn't learned any life skills from her punishment. She knows no more about alcohol use or why she needs to control it. She knows nothing about the consequences of drinking, only about the consequences of getting caught. She is completely focused on being angry with her parents, who now have zero ability to influence her. Punishment leads to feelings of hatred, revenge, defiance, and self-pity. It's a distraction to the learning process because the teen becomes pre-occupied with revenge fantasies. This is not a scenario from which they learn anything useful.

> *There is no better way to buy bad behaviour than to pay for good behaviour.*

How About Rewards Then?

Parents often think rewards are the way to go because they are positive and reinforcing. But frankly, there is no better way to buy bad behaviour than to pay for good behaviour.

> *For Example: Jeff's parents were convinced that the reason his grades were so poor was because he just wasn't trying. They knew how smart he was. So they told him that if he could bring his C- marks up to a C+, they'd give him $10 per C+. When Jeff proved them right by getting C+ marks, they told him he'd get $20 per B. When this worked, they got so excited they offered*

Reward and punishment encourage
manipulation and encourage the
idea that appropriate behaviour is
only necessary when an authority
figure is present.

him $50 per A. After several terms of excellent marks, his parents decided that Jeff had now learned how to study and they discontinued the "money for marks" program. It didn't take a month before Jeff's marks were back in the toilet. His parents were disappointed and bewildered. After all, they'd proved how smart he was. Why wasn't he trying?

For a teen to grow into an adult capable of taking care of himself, he needs to have developed his own internal motivations for behaving in certain ways. Jeff needs to be studying and doing well academically so that his own future is wide open and full of options. Too many teens think that they're studying to keep their parents happy. They don't get it. Jeff quit trying because his only motivation for getting good marks had been removed.

Jenny's decisions about drinking needs to be based on her own belief system about the effects of alcohol on her life. If she doesn't drink because she'll be punished if she's caught, she'll figure out ways not to get caught. If she doesn't drink because her father pays her not to drink, how long is he willing to keep up the payments? When he stops, will she have the knowledge and decision-making skills to make a good decision for herself?

If a parent rewards good behaviour and punishes bad behaviour, they make themselves responsible for their teen's behaviour. Reward and punishment also encourage manipulation and encourage the idea that appropriate behaviour is only necessary when an authority figure is present. Reward and punishment are not discipline. The goal of effective discipline is to provide the teen with the guidelines they need to take responsibility for their own behaviour.

But They're Too Young For That Kind of Responsibility!

Too young for what? To take responsibility for themselves? Responsibility is not a gift that's delivered at a pre-defined birthday. Responsible decision-making is learned, preferably from very early childhood.

> *For Example: When five-year-old Tod takes a bite out of his sandwich and discovers it's egg salad instead of the peanut butter he was expecting, he throws it to the ground and stomps on it. Now, one of two things will happen: either he learns that stomping his sandwich into the dirt makes it inedible and that means he will be hungry all afternoon or Mommy rushes in with a fresh sandwich and apologizes for giving him the wrong sandwich. Either he learns that tem-per tantrums and destructive behaviour cause uncomfortable consequences like hunger or he learns that every time he's displeased, he should behave badly and Mommy will rescue him.*

Children of all ages need to experience the genuine consequences of their own behaviour. This is where learning to make good and appropriate decisions for themselves begins.

NATURAL AND LOGICAL CONSEQUENCES

The natural consequence of a behaviour is the experience that follows naturally from that behaviour.

> *For Example: If I don't put gas in the car, it will run out of gas and I will walk.*

Natural consequences are life's very best teachers when:
- they won't injure or kill someone;
- their effects are immediate enough for the teen to comprehend; and
- the consequences of their behaviour won't affect others more than themselves.

When a parent cannot rely on natural consequences as the teacher, they can set up logical consequences as the next best teacher. Logical consequences are results that a parent sets up to show a teen what logically follows when the teen chooses a particular behaviour.

For Example: If the teen manages to get the car back into the garage without actually running out of gas, but the tank is on dead empty, the logical consequence might be that she may not use the car for two weeks.

This is not a punishment. It is the logical consequence of not returning an item to its place, ready for the next person's use. Of course, these family rules need to be agreed upon in advance, and the logical consequences of violating the rules also need to be clearly communicated. To be an effective teacher, logical consequences cannot be a surprise.

Involve the teen in the discussion about both the house rules and the consequences of violating those rules. Most kids have a keen sense of justice and will come up with creative consequences. They will also understand the logic of consequences that are as directly related to the behaviour as possible. The objective is for the teen to learn something about the results of their behaviour, not be punished. To do that, the focus needs to stay on the behaviour.

For Example: If Alec leaves a mess in the kitchen when he fixes himself and his friends snacks in the evening, Alec might lose kitchen privileges for two weeks. If Jenny persists in getting drunk, she loses the privilege of using the car until she learns to handle alcohol more responsibly (or quits, depending on family values). If Aaron takes some of his Dad's tools over to a friends house to fix a car and then loses them, he must pay for their replacement.

Sometimes it's very hard for a parent to let consequences be the teacher. I know that when one of my sons, who was a chronic "loser of things", left his prized bike at school and it was stolen, my immediate instinct was to help him replace it. But this was just one item in a long list of things that he'd "lost" and we believed we wouldn't be doing him a favour if we kept jumping in and replacing these things. But my heart almost broke, watching that little guy trudge off to school each day on foot. It took him about four months of delivering papers and yardwork, but he earned a new bike and in seven years, it's never been "lost".

Since Leon had experienced both the natural consequences of abusing alcohol and the logical consequences of drunkenness they were satisfied that he now understood the ramifications of his decision to drink.

Delivery

Punishment is often delivered in an atmosphere of anger and emotion, but the delivery of logical consequences should be handled in a low-key and firm-but-friendly manner. If the family has already discussed the issue and knows what the consequences of certain behaviours will be, there are no surprises. If you are surprised by a behaviour that you hadn't thought about before, tell your son or daughter that you need time to think. Don't make off-the-cuff decisions that may have long-term ramifications. If you need time, take it. Give them a time frame, "I need to think about this for an hour", or "until tomorrow", or "for a week". Ask them to think about it too and come up with some ideas.

> *For Example: John and Judith were on vacation, alone. One night their son Leon called their hotel from home. He and the friend he was staying with had decided to try drinking when the friend's parents were away. They'd only taken a little shot glass of each bottle of liqueur, but apparently these parents had an extensive collection of liqueurs and the boys had no understanding of their potency. The boys had gotten so drunk and so sick that they'd vomited all over the carpets and drapes. John and Judy's son was calling because, he was very, very anxious to know what the consequence would be. He wanted an answer right then on the phone. He desperately wanted to put this unhappy experience behind him and he wanted to know, immediately, what else was going to happen. His friend had been grounded for two months because of it. What was going to happen to him?*

> *Wisely, John and Judith told him that they were going to need to think about this and they'd discuss it with him when they returned home in two days. In the meantime, maybe he could think about it too.*

> *When they returned home, Leon reported that he and his friend had rented a carpet cleaner and spent the previous day cleaning the carpets. As well, they'd taken down the drapes which they'd splattered with vomit and taken them to the dry cleaners, where they were shocked to discover it was going to cost over $300 (all of Leon's savings) to clean them. They'd also laundered the bedding they'd soiled and cleaned up the furniture.*

> *Leon's parents were pleased with the way that he'd taken responsibility for cleaning up the mess he'd made. They explained that since Leon had experienced both the natural consequences of abusing alcohol (vomiting and a terrible hangover) and the logical consequences of drunkenness (cleaning up after themselves and the expenses involved) they were satisfied that he now understood the ramifications of his decision to drink. The matter was closed.*

*When our son heads out into a blizzard with nothing more than a
t-shirt, we wonder if tomorrow's headline is going to read,
"Fifteen-year-old Boy Freezes to Death Without Coat – Where
Were His Parents?"*

WHOSE PROBLEM IS IT ANYWAY?

Most parents begin the parenting journey with some ideas about what
makes a good parent.

> *For Example: A good parent makes sure their children do their
> homework. A good parent makes sure their children eat nutritious,
> healthy meals. A good parent makes sure their children wear warm,
> weatherproof clothes in bad weather.*

Sound reasonable? Not once our children hit adolescence. Then all
these issues can become battlegrounds for power. Our teens' push for

independence runs smack into our need to be a "good parent".

We all feel it. When the school calls to tell us that Jed is flunking out of math, we feel that we should do something. If we got on his case a little more, he'd study more. Right?

When our daughter quits eating meat and turns into a beanpole, it's very hard not to feel criticized when Aunt Emily remarks, "Aren't you feeding this girl anything? Send her over to my house. I'll fatten her up alright!"

When our teenage son heads out into a full-scale blizzard refusing to wear anything more than a t-shirt, we wonder if tomorrow's headline is going to read, "Fifteen-year-old Boy Freezes to Death Without Coat – Where Were His Parents?"

Although we feel responsible for our teens, it's not reasonable for a good parent to think they can make their teen do anything. What a good parent *can* do is provide:

- a quiet, comfortable place for them to do their homework;
- nutritious food and information about how to plan a healthy diet that's appropriate to the teen's objectives; and
- clothing that's appropriate to the weather conditions.

What bothers you?

Make a list of all the things that bother you about your teen's behaviour.

For example:
Won't eat breakfast.
Doesn't return my tools.
Loses his belongings.
Is always late.
Leaves dishes in the family room.
Stays up late.

Now take each item and decide whether it's really a teen problem, a parent problem or some of both.

For Example: Won't eat breakfast.

Food is the classic battleground between kids and parents. It starts in early childhood (when swallowing and defecating are the only things a child controls) and, if the parent keeps playing the game, will continue until one of you dies. Healthy kids don't starve to death. If she's hungry, she'll eat. Stay out of it. If you suspect an eating disorder, nagging will not fix it (see *Chapter Twelve*). Parents can make sure there is nutritious food in the house and they can be responsive to a teen's desire to try a different way of eating (like vegetarianism) but eating or not eating is definitely something that teens control and parents will get nowhere nagging about it.

For Example: Doesn't return my tools.

Since not returning your tools affects you, it is definitely a parent problem. Fortunately, the logical consequence required to cure this problem behaviour is simple. If something is not returned, the borrower may not use it for an agreed-upon length of time. Be calm, but firm. There is nothing to argue about.

For Example: Loses his belongings.

 Losing things is definitely a teen problem, unless, your teen expects you to replace them. That, then, becomes your problem, but the solution is very simple. Give notice that you won't be replacing things your teen loses and then don't. There are always opportunities for teens to earn money – mowing lawns, shovelling snow, delivering papers, or flipping burgers.

For Example: Is always late.

If you are letting your teen's chronic "lateness" affect your own life, then it's become your problem. Make sure it *isn't* your problem by serving notice that you will no longer wait past the appointed time. If your son or daughter misses the school bus, let *them* worry about it. If they're late for work or team games or lessons, let them explain. This is only your problem if you make it your problem. Constantly nagging them, driving them to school when they miss the bus, and explaining and apologizing to coaches and teachers for them, is not doing your teen any favours. They need to deal with the consequences of their own behaviour themselves.

For Example: Leaves dishes in the family room.

Since your teen obviously isn't bothered by dirty dishes, it is your problem. In a family council meeting, talk about why this bothers you and discuss what the logical consequences of leaving dishes in the family room will be. Then be prepared to conform as well. If the logical consequence of leaving dishes in the family room is that the "leaver" cannot eat in the family room for a week, make sure you grab your coffee cup too!

Once you start pulling apart the things that bother you about your teen's behaviour, you will be amazed at how many things just aren't your problem. There is so much less to fight over!

Turning Over Responsibility

Nagging from now until sundown will not turn your teen into a good student.

As a parent, it is very hard to let go of some of those areas of responsibility (like supervising homework) that you've always believed were your responsibility. If you realize, though, that nagging from now until sundown will not turn your teen into a good student, it will be easier. That does not mean you shouldn't say anything. Far from it.

When you've decided that it's time to turn your teen's problems back over to her, choose a time when you're both calm and rested to talk about it. Sit her down and calmly explain the situation.

> *For Example: "I have spent your school years trying to make you study. I've always believed that what you did once you finished school would be up to you, but I also knew that if your marks were good, you would have so many more options from which to choose. I wanted a future for you that was wide open and full of choices. I now realize that I cannot make you study or do well in school. Only you can do that for yourself. It is your life and if you choose to limit your options that's your choice too.*
>
> *I now realize that decisions about studying and whether or not to complete homework are best made by you, for yourself. If you ask, I will always try to help you, but I will not be harassing you about homework or researching your essays or typing papers at two in the morning anymore."*
>
> *End by reassuring her again that you are confident she will make good decisions for herself and that you are really looking forward to the improved relationship the two of you will enjoy now that you are getting out of areas of her life that belong to her.*

Now the hard part begins, make certain to stay out of it.

> *Work out the negotiables while you're
> calm and the discussion is all in the realm
> of the theoretical.*

Preventing Problems

Identify potential problem areas (like a teen getting their driver's licence) long before they happen and set guidelines and consequences while everyone is still calmly and happily anticipating this next step in your teen's life.

Together, brainstorm what the issues will be. For example, who pays for gas, accidents and repairs? Are there any geographical boundaries on where your teen can or cannot drive? Can your teen drive friends around? What about drinking or drug use and driving?

Make a clear distinction between the things that are negotiable (like paying for repairs) and those things that are non-negotiable (like drinking and driving). Sit down as a family and work out the negotiables together while you're calm and the discussion is all in the realm of the theoretical.

Make sure everyone knows the rules and their consequences. Write them down. Many parents find it helpful, for instance, to write a "driving contract" with their teen. Think about it.

Anger

No one is as well equipped to make their parent crazy as an adolescent son or daughter. After twelve, fourteen or sixteen years of intimate family living, they know so well, where all our hot buttons are. Since at this age they are intrinsically self-centred, they will push every one if they believe there is any chance it will get them what they want.

If you do lose your temper, explain later. Don't think it will go away and everyone will forget about it. They won't. If you get mad and send your teen to their room, it gets them out of your face, which solves your problem, but it doesn't solve theirs.

If you get mad and send your teen to their room, it gets them out of your face, which solves your problem, but it doesn't solve theirs.

The most helpful piece of advice I was ever given was that I shouldn't allow myself to be pushed into making decisions when I'm angry. Take the time to truly consider the long-term ramifications of any decision you make.

Conflict Resolution

Once parents realize how so many of the things they used to fight about simply aren't their problem anymore, and they learn how to stay out of these areas (biting your tongue is a big part of this), the level of conflict in a home goes way down.

But some conflict, there will always be. If there weren't, it would mean that were no differences of opinion, and no independent thinking going on. Conflict is part of every normal, healthy relationship. That doesn't mean, though, that it isn't stressful. Fortunately, the Conflict Resolution Process thoroughly described in *Chapter Seven* will help you put the emphasis on the problem, not the people.

SOME FINAL THOUGHTS

Threatening kids with punishment that you've no intention of enforcing destroys your credibility with them. Keep the "consequences" realistic and related to the behaviour; then follow through. Avoid empty threats.

Once you've made decisions about rules and consequences, stay calm and neutral. Don't get sucked into arguing about things that have already been decided. If you are disappointed and upset that your teen has done poorly in school or lost a job because they showed up late for work too often, be sympathetic but detached. Express confidence in their ability to do what's best for themselves in the future.

For Example: "Oh, I'm sorry you lost that job. You were really look-ing forward to buying a car, weren't you? Oh well, I'm sure you'll remember to set your alarm the next time you get a job. I know you can do it."

Remember too, that expectations influence results.

For Example: If a parent were to say something like: "If I let you stay overnight at Tyler's you'll just get into trouble anyway," they are influencing the results. If the kids get into trouble, doesn't that prove the parent right? Don't parents always want to be right?

If kids are told they are losers, they become losers. Positive expecta-tions are more likely to yield more positive results.

Before you get too overwrought and angry about something your teen has done, take a deep breath and calmly talk it over with them. They are often so lost in their own self-centred little world that they don't even know what they've done wrong. They could well repeat the same behav-iour and still wouldn't know they'd done anything wrong. Talk to them.

Respect your teens and show them respect by the way you talk to them. Too often, teenagers get treated so disrespectfully and offensively that the only logical reaction is rebellion.

For Example: When Dad, in a hurry, gets out to the car to run fif-teen-year-old Josh over to his soccer game, he finds Josh in the dri-ver's seat, blissfully pretending that he is a driver in the Indy 500. "What the hell you think you're doing? We're late already as it is. Get your butt out of my seat before I do it for you!!!!!"

We wouldn't tolerate the same kind of behaviour from our teens toward us, would we? If you're feeling tense, think of your kids as work colleagues or customers in your shop, or clients at a sales meeting. Just treat them like real people. It's not too much to ask.

~ Chapter Twelve ~

MENTAL HEALTH

The Best Years of Their Lives?

Long ago, someone proclaimed "youth" to be the best years of our lives. That belief stuck and is replayed in reruns, part of our North American mythology. When we ask adults about this, a few here and there, the prom queens and basketball stars of their youth, will agree, but most people get a sad smile on their face and disagree. Adolescence was not the happiest of times for us.

Adolescence is so packed with tasks and traumas that it is probably the most stressful period of our lives. It's not surprising, then, that during the teen years we are most vulnerable to depression and thoughts of suicide, the second leading cause of death for teens. Only accidents account for more, and it is believed that many accidents are really disguised or unreported suicides.

> *Suicide is the second leading cause of death for teens. Only accidents account for more, and it is believed that many accidents are really disguised or unreported suicides.*

Why are teens so vulnerable to depression?

There is an incredible amount of "growing up work" to be done during the teen years. Children come into adolescence as just that, children. They are dependent on their parents for everything from the bed they sleep in,

If they've had little experience with the decision-making process, they will probably make lots of mistakes. Instead of feeling empowered and proud of themselves, they will feel like failures.

to reminders to brush their teeth.

When they leave adolescence just a few, short years later, they are adults, who are expected to provide for themselves and know how to run their lives effectively. The evolution from child to adult is dramatic and must be accomplished in a very short period of time.

If independence and autonomy have always been encouraged, teens have a head start in accepting personal responsibility. They will have had many opportunities to make age-appropriate decisions.

For Example: Even young children can choose which t-shirt to wear or whether they would prefer apple or orange juice for breakfast.

Too often, however, parents make virtually all their children's decisions for them – from what they wear, to who their friends are to what they eat.

Once the hormonal tsunami hits, kids struggle really hard against this level of parental involvement in their lives. They will insist on making their own decisions. But if they've had little experience with the decision-making process, they won't be very good at it and will probably make lots of mistakes. Instead of feeling empowered and proud of themselves, they will feel like failures. And no doubt there'll be a chorus of critics to point out how badly they're screwing up.

THE "WORK" OF ADOLESCENCE

Professionals who study how we grow and develop say that there are four main tasks adolescents need to accomplish if they are to make a healthy transition to adulthood:

1. Determine Their Vocation
2. Develop Their Own Values
3. Explore Their Sexuality
4. Establish Their Own Authority

1. Determining Their Vocation

What will they do with their lives? One's "job", whatever it might be, gives meaning to one's life. It's where we fit into the world, whether as a factory line worker, office clerk, nurse, or supreme court judge. There is also a culture associated with different vocations and different workplaces and since we spend so much of our waking lives at work and with colleagues pursuing the same vocation, this culture plays a major role in defining who we are.

There is a culture associated with different vocations, and it plays a major role in defining who we are.

For Example: Bonny is a legal secretary at a big, downtown law firm. She works a Monday-to-Friday, 9-to-5 schedule, spends a lot of her income on dressing well, and generally pursues a very urban lifestyle.

Moira is a big-animal veterinarian. She spends her work day in boots and jeans and her time off hanging out at horse shows. She lives simply, saving money for the ranch she expects to own in the future.

Jeff is an airline mechanic. He wears the company uniform and takes full advantage of the free travel, which enables him to see the world. Jeff works shift work and is an enthusiastic participant in the league sports that his workplace organizes.

A job is never just a job. It's a determining factor in helping us sort out who we are.

Our pay cheques are also our routes to independence, to fulfilling our own unique desires. Are we a musician or skier or movie fan or traveller

Even looking for a part-time job is a traumatic experience, fraught with rejection. Remember?

or antique buff or race car driver or perennial student? Each of these pursuits take money and that means finding a job that, if it is not fulfilling in itself, provides the funds for us to find fulfilment elsewhere.

When we are thwarted in this area, say by being refused entry to an educational program we need to complete our qualifications, or by not being able to find a good job, we experience emotions like rejection, isolation, and alienation. Determining a vocation is a major developmental task of adolescence and in today's tight economy in which companies are downsizing and educational institutions have restricted entrance to only the top students, this decision is a major cause of anxiety and stress. Even looking for a part-time job is a traumatic experience, fraught with rejection. Remember?

2. Developing Their Own Values

What values and beliefs will teens assimilate from their family and what will they discard? Throughout their lives, teens' parents have imposed their own values in relation to issues like: religious affiliation; use of alcohol and drugs; work ethic; patriotism; education; and sexual activity. With the increasing freedom of adolescence and their increasing resistance to accepting anything holus-bolus, teens review these values for relevance in their own lives. They develop their own set of beliefs.

Expect your teens to challenge your values and, also, to experiment with other values. Sometimes they'll try a new idea on and strut around for a day or two, enjoying the shock value. If parents can stay low key and non-judgemental, saying "It's an option", a teen won't have to defend a new belief too vigorously, and will often abandon it quite quickly and move on to something else. If a parent has been very vocal about putting down the teen's new belief, however, it becomes very difficult for a rebellious teen to back down, even when they want to.

Take comfort in the fact that most of us, by the time we are adults, have internalized the values of our upbringing and live out our lives, for better or for worse, following the same values our parents did.

When teens are not able to work through this task, they stay mixed up and unsure of what they believe in, always a little lost.

> *If a parent has been vocal about putting down the teen's new belief, however, it becomes very difficult for a rebellious teen to back down, even when they want to.*

3. Exploring Their Sexuality

What does it mean to be man or a woman?

Although sexual experimentation is certainly a part of this issue, it goes beyond that to the fundamentals of sexuality. What does it mean to be a man or a woman and how do I fit into that great cosmic family of men or women?

Society send us lots of messages about what real men or real women do. Sometimes these messages don't fit with our own understanding of ourselves. If our culture tells us that tall, generously muscled men with hairy chests are real men, how do we fit if genetics have created us short and skinny? What if real women this year are big breasted and have long, straight hair, but we're flat chested and have hair that curls like a brillo pad?

These are just the exterior features. What about the internal attitudes and emotions that so many of us find just don't fit with the norm? Our society tells us that real men love to watch sports on television.

What if we just don't fit in.

What if you're a teenage boy who's bored to death by sports and would rather play the piano. Are you still a real man? What if all the girls we know spend their free time doing and re-doing their hair and makeup while they gossip endlessly about boys, but we're bored to tears by this? We'd rather be rock climbing. Do real women climb mountains?

Parents of teens who are "different" can help them navigate this area of adolescence by finding adult role models with interests similar to their teens' for them to take strength from and the reassurance that real men and real women do pursue interests outside the mainstream.

Adolescence is also quite often a time of confusion around sexual orientation. Most teens, at one time or another, are attracted to someone of the same sex. This doesn't mean they are homosexual. Such same-sex attractions are normal, but the experience can be very confusing for teens. Teens need to know that homosexuality is a *longstanding* and *long-term* preference for the same sex.

Society doesn't make life easy for homosexuals.

Of course, our teen may be homosexual, in which case they need even more help accepting themselves and their place in the world. Most of us don't believe that homosexuality is a choice people make: it is pre-ordained at birth and not something the person can change about themselves. But society still doesn't make life easy for homosexuals. As parents, we can do *nothing* to influence sexual orientation, but we can accept it as something that simply *is*. Our openness to discussion will certainly make our teens' lives easier. Many of their peers will ostracize them, so make home the place they belong and are valued, just for being them.

Heterosexual or homosexual, teens need to use the years of adolescence to become comfortable with their own personal definition of what it is to be a man or a woman.

4. Establish Their Own Authority

Children look, their whole lives, toward their parents to provide them the security of an authority figure. They are told when to go to bed, what to eat, when to go to the dentist, what vitamin supplements to take, whether a situation is safe or unsafe, when they are old enough to cross the road alone, and when they are sick enough to see a doctor. In families in which the parenting is conscientious and caring, this makes for a very secure world. While the nature of kids as they get older is to push the limits of parental authority, and it's good that they do or most of use would still be walking our 16 year-olds to school, they know that if Mom or Dad is adamant about the "No" then it probably is an unsafe situation. Similarly if they relent, then "It must be okay, 'cause Mom said it was."

Too often, when parents are too firmly at the decision-making helm, their children never really experience failure. They're not familiar with the emotion or how immobilizing it can be.

Travelling through adolescence means taking over this decision making for themselves and, while they put a brave, even arrogant face on it, being responsible for ourselves is scary. Wise parents hand over this responsibility in incremental, but steadily progressive steps so that the mistakes, when they come, are not life threatening.

An introduction to "failure" is not a bad thing either. Too often, when parents are too firmly at the decision-making helm, their children never really experience failure. They're not familiar with the emotion or how immobilizing it can be. When the inevitable happens and they do fail at something, they're devastated. They doubt their own ability to take care of themselves and may be immobilized by the fear of making decisions for themselves.

Let your teens discover failure in situations that are *not* life shattering. The experience will encourage self-evaluation: looking at what didn't work and why. They need to learn how to pick themselves back up and give something another go. They need to know that just because they feel like a failure today, it won't always be so, and that *they* are the ones in control of how long it will be until they feel like winners again.

Adolescence is a time to work through all of these issues and the process can be difficult and painful. While everyone experiences this pain, not everyone grows from it, however. Growth requires us to struggle through the pain, not bury it or hide from it or run away from it. Teens who get involved in alcohol or drug abuse are running from their pain and these substances so anaesthetize them that they don't work through the developmental tasks of adolescence.

Self Esteem Fluctuates

Experiencing low self esteem is not unusual for a teenager and levels of self esteem can swing widely from day to day.

> *For Example: Consider the young adolescent graduating from elementary school. In his school, he's cock-of-the-walk, king of the mountain, one of the graduating movers and shakers. A few days later, trembling with trepidation he approaches the high school for his first day as one of the lowliest of the low, a grade eight nobody. He is now unworthy, unwanted, and unwelcome, the butt of all the bullies above him. What a difference a day can make!*

A teen's sense of personal identity is reflected back to them by others. These messages play a large part in defining who they are, but during the teen years, these messages can be mixed. Teens need to work through the negative messages and learn that they don't have to be devastated by them. But it is a painful experience.

As a parent, one wants to make everything better for their child, but this is one of the areas in which the parent of a teen begins to understand their limitations.

> *For Example: If one of the hot girls at school has just made the hallway group laugh by making a joke at Jordan's expense (big nose, long arms, breaking voice, glasses) it will not matter how many times Mom says Jordan is handsome. Mom's opinion in this just doesn't count anymore.*

What can parents do? Not much directly. And that is acutely painful for us. We can support our kids and tell them stories about what geeks we were in high school, but since our teens probably think we're real geeks now, the stories don't hold out any reassurance of a better tomorrow!

**Since our teens probably think we're still geeks,
our high school horror stories won't provide
any reassurance of a better tomorrow!**

Indirectly we can help our teens build confidence in themselves and pride in themselves – everything we talk about in this book is directed at doing just that. We can facilitate their participation in activities that highlight their strengths, whether that be music or hockey or drama or gymnastics. These activities offer them opportunities for success, proof that they *can* do something right. We can commiserate with them, never belittling their painful emotions or their attempts to fit into the school social scene. And finally, we can ensure that they have a place, home, where they are accepted and loved unconditionally.

No Perspective on Depression

Teens are often experiencing depression for the first time and they don't have the perspective of age. Adults know that these feelings will pass, but a teen who is experiencing depression for the first time doesn't have that perspective to work from. They believe that how they are feeling at the moment is how it will always be and that thought may be unbearable.

At the same time we assure teens that feelings of depression will pass, it is very important that we do not trivialize them. Suicidal teens often feel that their emotions are belittled by those around them. Something that may seem trivial and temporary to a parent may be devastating to the teen, and it is very important that we respect that.

Parents need to know that there are basically two kinds of depression. Reactive depression is the kind that occurs in response to a loss. It is how we feel when someone we love leaves us or dies , when we lose a job, or when we aren't admitted to a program we need to get into. Once we work though the grief associated with this loss, it normally goes away.

Endogenous depression appears for no apparent reason and seems to be internally generated. It lasts longer than a few weeks and seems to go on without end. It often causes the person to engage in risky behaviour or consider suicide. These people often turn to alcohol and drugs to escape but, in fact, such substances actually deepen depression. If you

What makes suicidally prone teens different from other teens is the way in which they react to their difficulties.

believe that your teen is suffering from this kind of depression, seek professional help. Some studies show that one in ten teens will attempt suicide by the time they finish high school. Depression is serious and you'll need help.

Recognizing Teens at Risk

Suicidal teens come from all socio-economic and cultural groups. What makes suicidally prone teens different from other teens is the way in which they react to their difficulties. What may be only temporarily upsetting to another teen is devastating to them. They often feel hopeless and helpless to change things. While more girls than boys attempt suicide, six times as many boys complete a suicide. It is believed this is because boys tend to choose more lethal methods.

There is no suicidal personality type, but the presence of the following factors make a teen more vulnerable and consequently at greater risk of attempting suicide:

Risk Factors

- **low self-esteem**
  A teen may believe they are weak and cowardly for even thinking about suicide. If they have low self esteem and feel worthless already, they are caught in a vicious cycle that makes them vulnerable to suicidal thoughts.

- **feeling helpless or hopeless**
  Suicidal teens feel that whatever is making them unhappy is beyond their control to change. The only power they believe they have, is the power to end the pain by killing themselves.

- **in trouble**
  These teens just can't seem to do anything right. They are in trouble with the law, their school, and their parents. They have a short fuse and are very impulsive. They are often desperate for a way out.

- **abused**

  Even years after the abuse has ended, victims of abuse can be overwhelmed by feelings of shame, guilt, and isolation.

- **perfectionists**

  Although teens who are perfectionists usually look very success-ful, they never quite measure up in their own eyes. They under-value their own achievements and even a small setback can be devastating to them.

- **homosexual**

  Life is not kind to homosexual teens as they are more likely to suffer rejection, discrimination, and isolation.

- **experienced a traumatic event or recent loss**

  The causes of suicide are usually deeply rooted and longstand-ing, but a crisis can be the "final straw" that moves a teen into deciding to kill him or herself.

- **abuses alcohol or drugs**

  Alcohol and drugs simply make matters worse.

- **disabled**

  Teens with disabilities are often unaccepted, discouraged, alien-ated from their peers, and worried about the future.

- **loner - socially isolated**

  Everyone needs a friend, and when teens have difficulty relating to their peers, they are missing an important source of support.

- **recent suicide of family member or friend**

  When teens are overwhelmed with feelings of grief, helplessness, and guilt, the bereaved often play with the idea of suicide them-selves. The suicide of their family member or friend's suicide may make it look to them as if suicide is an acceptable option out of painful situations. They are at high risk of suicide.

Warning Signs

Although a single, traumatic event can trigger an unexpected suicide, most teens send out signals such as:

- talking or joking about suicide;
- increasing their use of alcohol or drugs;
- making final arrangements such as giving away prized possessions; or
- taking reckless risks.

Teens may also exhibit sudden changes in their personality or attitudes such as:
- abrupt changes in school attendance
- sudden decline in academic performance
- inability to concentrate
- sudden failure to complete school assignments
- lack of interest and withdrawal
- changed relationship with friends
- increased irritability or aggressiveness
- wide mood swings
- unexpected displays of emotion
- despairing attitude
- preoccupation with death and suicide (for example: writing about it, or drawing pictures of people committing suicide or dead)
- a party animal becomes withdrawn or vice versa
- disturbed sleep, loss of appetite
- loss of interest in previously important relationships
- appearance and personal care change suddenly

Suicidal teens feel helpless, hopeless, and are in a great deal of pain. They don't usually want to kill themselves; they just want the pain to end. This is the key to helping them.

*A teen who is experiencing depression believes that how they
are feeling at the moment is how it will always be and that
may be unbearable.*

HOW TO HELP

When you initiate a conversation with a teen by asking them what's
wrong, you'll probably be met with a shrug and a muttered, "Nothing."
Don't give up. Before they'll open up and talk to you they'll probably
need to be convinced that you really care and really are prepared to listen
to them. Here are some openers to try:

"I've noticed that you seem down about
    something."

"You seem to want to be alone a lot."

"You look like you're unhappy about
    something."

"Can you tell me what's making you
    unhappy?"

"There must be something serious troubling you, for you to
    look this down."

*The single most
common complaint
by teens about
adults is that we
don't listen.*

The best way to find out if someone is thinking about committing suicide is simply to ask them directly. This does not put ideas into their head, but it does free them to talk about what is really going on for them.

The single most common complaint by teens about adults is that we don't listen. When teens do confide their problems in us, our natural-born need to solve their problems causes us to jump in with advice about what they should or should not do. This is not listening.

Once they start talking, try to listen without making judgments or giving advice. This delivers three very important messages:

1) I take your problems seriously.
2) I care enough about you to want to help.
3) I have faith in your ability to figure this out.

To keep the conversation going, use phrases like:

"Tell me about it."

"What are you feeling now?"

"What happened then?"

"What worries you the most?"

"That sounds rough."

Be alert for words and phrases that suggest suicidal intentions, like "I'd rather die than go back to school", or "I can't take it anymore", or "Everybody would be better off if I wasn't around." These are not jokes, they are strong hints about what is going on in his or her head.

Don't tell the teen what to do, but do share your feelings. Tell him you can see how unhappy he is and that this makes you very anxious. Tell him or her: "I can see why you're feeling the way you are, but there are other solutions. I'd like to help you look for a way out of your pain."

At times everyone feels sad, hurt, or confused. If you can relate to how your teen is feeling, say so. If there was a time when your whole world was in ruins, share it, but be very honest. Teens have highly developed bullshit sensors. They'll know if you're stretching the truth and you'll lose both your credibility and your ability to help.

> ## *Means + Availablity + Plan = RISK*

Evaluate the Risk

The best way to find out if someone is thinking about committing suicide is simply to ask them directly. "Are you thinking about killing yourself?"

This does not put ideas into their head, but it does free them to talk about what is really going on for them and to reach out for help.

If they answer "Yes," ask them:
"What method have you thought of using to kill yourself?"
"When do you think you'll do this?"
"Do have the means (guns, pills, etc.)?"

Risk: The more dangerous the method, the more available the method and the more definite the plan, the greater the risk is that they'll attempt suicide.

Get Help

Don't ever agree to keep someone's suicide plans a secret. Try to find out who and what they fear, and if possible look for help elsewhere, but do not keep suicidal intentions a secret. It is better to have a mad teen than a dead teen. If, in your opinion, the risk of a suicide attempt is high (means + availability + plan), DO NOT LEAVE THEM ALONE until help arrives.

Help in a Crisis Situation
- emergency wards
- police or ambulance
- Kids Helpline 1-800-668-6868
- local Crisis Line or Centre
- doctor
- school counsellor
- friend or neighbour

A doctor will probably prescribe medication that will take the edge off your teen's emotional pain. While this is helpful and will probably reduce the risk that he or she will attempt suicide in the short term, it will not resolve the deep and longstanding problems that led this teen to this place in their lives. The danger is not over, he or she is still very much at risk. He/she will need counselling to help them resolve pain and get back to the business of growing up. The developmental work that an emotionally healthy teen has to do is formidable. The work that a suicidal teen has to do can be overwhelming. They need help.

CONNECTING WITH A COUNSELLOR

The profession of "counselling" is, in most senses, unregulated. Anyone can hang out a shingle and offer their services, so it's necessary to be aware and ask lots of questions. Good and not-so-good counsellors can be found in each of the counselling professions:.

Psychiatrists

Psychiatrists are medical doctors with specific training in emotional and psychological problems. Psychiatrists can prescribe medication.

Psychologists

With either a doctorate or a master's degree in counselling psychology, psychologists are registered with a College of Psychologists.

Counsellors

Clergy, social workers, psychiatric nurses, school counsellors, emergency ward, and crisis centre counsellors, as well as people trained in counselling techniques who work for half-way houses, detox centres, transition houses, group homes, and so on.

How to Find Help?

- Your medical doctor can refer to either a psychiatrist or a psychologist.
- If your place of employment has an Employee Assistance Program, it will often have counsellors on retainer that you and your dependants may see as part of your benefit package.
- Community and Family Service Agencies - Either have counsellors on staff or can refer you to good counsellors. They will likely also know

which counselling organizations in the community work on a sliding scale according to income.

- Mental Health Offices - Have counsellors on staff.
- Counselling Organizations - These organizations employ and supervise counsellors and often offer a sliding scale according to income.
- Clergy - If you are affiliated with a religious organization, it is worth "talking to your clergy" as these people can often be well-trained counsellors. Large religious institutions often employ counsellors just for the purpose of counselling.
- Yellow pages of your telephone directory - look under "Counselling".

A Good Connection

There is more, however, to finding a good counsellor than just making an appointment. For counselling to be effective, it's important to find a good fit for you and your teen.

There are many philosophies or schools of thought on human behaviour and different counsellors conduct their practice according to the philosophies they believe in. There are counsellors, for instance, who believe that the source of conflict is found in our family history and that we need to untangle the stuff that's happened in our families before we can move forward. Others believe that people's emotions are controlled by their views and opinions of the world. They believe that if we change our beliefs, we will change how we feel and so they concentrate on changing negative thought patterns. There are other counsellors who are into new-age stuff like reading auras and use scented oils and candles in their practice.

It's important that you find a counsellor whose belief system makes sense to you and your teen. They should be able to explain to both of you, in good, basic English, where they're coming from in terms of therapy. If you're not satisfied with their explanation or it just doesn't make sense to either of you, find another counsellor.

It's also important to follow your gut instinct in the matter of "personalities". You and your teen need to be able to really trust this person so, in this area, things like personality, age, and gender are very important. If either of you feel uncomfortable with a counsellor or if you just don't like them, then find another counsellor. Remember though, that

It's important that you find a counsellor whose belief system makes sense to you and your teen.

while you will be involved in some of the counselling sessions, it is probable that most of the sessions will be between your teen and the counsellor. Rely most heavily on your teen's feelings about the counsellor. It is most important that they feel they can trust and work with this person.

It is not unusual for people to have initial appointments with two or three counsellors before they feel, instinctively, that the chemistry is right. It is worth persevering as a good counselling relationship can mean, literally, the difference between life and death for some teens.

Remember that you are employing them, so start by telephoning prospective counsellors and questioning them. If anyone isn't interested in answering your questions, strike them from your list immediately.

Choosing a Counsellor

Some questions you might ask them:

1. What are your qualifications and training?
2. Are you a member of any professional associations?
3. What kind of experience do you have working with teens?
4. What approach do you take to counselling? Where are you coming from philosophically? (Make sure they explain this to you in language that is understandable. Ask as many questions as it takes to ensure you understand their belief system.)
5. Is your practice associated with any counselling organizations or groups?
6. How often and for how long do you see clients?
7. What are your fees?
8. What are your hours or work and where is your office located?

Don't be afraid to press for answers. Remember, you will be employing them.

*In a world that demands thinness as the feminine ideal, it is not
strange or crazy for young women to be trying to alter their bodies.*

EATING DISORDERS

It has been reported that 1% of school girls have anorexia nervosa and
10% are bulimic. While these disorders are not common in boys, they do
occur, so parents of both sexes need to keep their eyes open.

Anorexia Nervosa
Anorexia nervosa is characterized as:
1) refusal to maintain a minimal normal body weight
2) a fear of becoming fat even when visibly underweight
3) a very distorted body image
4) no menstrual cycles for at least three months in girls who've begun
   menstruation or the failure to begin menses in girls who should have
   begun menstruating

Bulimia Nervosa

Bulimia nervosa is characterized as:

1) a hatred of one's own body shape and weight
2) regular episodes of uncontrolled binge eating (vast quantities of food in a short period of time)
3) feeling out of control when binge eating
4) purging by any or several of the following methods: self-induced vomiting; laxatives; diuretics; excessive exercise; strict dieting; fasting

In a world that demands thinness as the feminine ideal, it is not strange or crazy for young women to be trying to alter their bodies. Studies show that at any given time, half of North American women are dieting and 80% dislike their bodies. Magazines and television programming actually organize women all over the world to try the same diets, desire the same body shape (pencil thin), squeeze into the same clothes, buy the same diet products and opt into the same mind set that you can never be too thin. Thinness is sold as the key to happiness, success, great relationships, and good times.

We all buy into this, commenting as we do on a friend or colleague's weight loss, "Oh you look so great!" The implication being, that they didn't look so great before. As a society, we have developed an abhorrence of fat and our children absorb this value as they grow up.

This preoccupation with attaining the socially approved body shape is where eating disorders are conceived. Adolescence, a time when maintaining one's self esteem is a daily struggle, is when it grows into a monster.

Is an eating disorder serious? Yes, very serious. Left untreated many girls don't "grow out of it". They do a great deal of damage to their bodies and even die.

While not eating or binging and purging may start out as freely made choices, the element of choice quickly disappears. These behaviours come to dominate the girl's life and she loses control very quickly.

Warning Signs

• Excessive Concern With Weight

These teens are pre-occupied with their body, constantly making critical remarks about themselves and trying new diet plans and weight-loss regimes. They are constantly battling their natural "set point" (the natural, internally set weight range for their body). They refuse to stop dieting and probably weigh themselves several times a day.

• Perfectionism

These teens believe that with more effort they will achieve perfection, not only in their body, but in other things like academic performance. This drive for perfection is more important than family or friends.

• Excessive Exercising

Among teens with eating disorders, it is common to exercise several hours per day, past the point of safety to the heart, skeleton, and muscles. They ignore the signs that would make most of us stop – dizziness, fainting, cold and blue extremities, and joint and muscle pain.

• Preoccupation With Food

Because many people with eating disorders are starving, they are constantly thinking about food. The disorder may not let them eat or retain the food they cook, but it is common for them to study cookbooks and prepare wonderful meals for their families. Girls with eating disorders will either deny they are hungry and refuse to eat, or eat but make a trip to the bathroom shortly after eating. People with eating disorders may also alternate strict dieting with binge eating. They will probably be secretive about the binging.

• Self-induced Vomiting

Repeated incidents of vomiting causes severe damage to the esophagus.

• Use of Laxatives, Diuretics, and Diet Pills

Overuse of laxatives and diuretics purge our bodies of the substances it needs to regulate important organ function.

If the diagnosis is, "She's just going through a phase", or "She'll grow out of it", find another doctor. Trust your hunch about this.

• Vegetarianism

Vegetarianism can be a healthy choice if attention is paid to ensuring an adequate intake of complete proteins, fats and carbohydrates, but those with eating disorders often use it as a cover to avoid eating either altogether, or anything that is calorie-rich like meat or cheese. Vegetarianism is also used as a cover for the adoption of bizarre food rituals.

• Mood Swings, Sleep, and Concentration

When we don't get the nutrients our bodies need, we undergo physiological changes that make it hard to sleep, concentrate, or do things that require stamina. Depression and mood swings are common byproducts.

When a female body is starved, menstruation stops, or, in the case of a very young girl, may not start. The likelihood of osteoporosis is also increased.

What You Can do

First and foremost, trust your own instincts about this. You know your own teen and are in the best position to observe changes in behaviour or body. Early intervention is the best treatment, but that said, be prepared to have your concern met with anger and denial by your teen. However, expressing concern for her health will leave the door open for discussion and will make it easier for her to consider getting help.

Express your love and pride in her often, without tying these expressions to discussions about her eating or weight. She desperately needs to feel accepted and nagging will definitely not help. Make sure you are not

*Encourage each member of
the family to keep living their
lives to the fullest.*

sending mixed messages (like going on a diet yourself).

Start by talking to her; then see your family doctor. If the diagnosis is, "She's just going through a phase", or "She'll grow out of it", find another doctor. Trust yourself and your hunch about this. Many parents of teens with eating disorders relate that this kind of dismissive response meant precious months were lost waiting while their teen became emaciated enough for their doctor to take them seriously.

Educate yourself by contacting organizations that are concerned with eating disorders (ask for addresses at your local library). Contact them and find out what treatment options are available in your area. Discuss those options with your doctor, including your teen in all these discussions. Find a counsellor who works specifically with clients who have eating disorders. Question the counsellor thoroughly to make sure they have experience in this area (see information about counsellors in previous pages). Your contacts with eating disorder organizations may have names of therapists who are particularly good in this area.

Once your teen is in treatment, avoid getting in discussions or arguments over weight and food behaviours. If you become concerned about her weight loss or other signs of medical problems, contact her doctor and her counsellor.

Don't let your whole life or your family's life become consumed by the eating disorder. Participate in family therapy or join a support group to help you work through your emotions. Take care of your own and your family's needs. Encourage each member of the family to keep living their lives to the fullest. It is very easy to become so enmeshed in one member's problems that the whole family is brought down. This is not helpful to the person with the eating disorder. If anything, it will make her feel guilty and that will exacerbate the condition. It will certainly not make her recovery happen one day faster.

LIVING WITH THE PAIN OF A TEEN WHO IS TROUBLED

There can't be anything more difficult for a parent than knowing their child is in pain. During the teen years, as in the adult years that follow, the parent's role is often to wait and watch while our teens work things out for themselves.

When you have done all that you can do, you must then turn your attention back onto yourself. Keeping yourself strong and healthy is very important both for yourself and your teen.

A few suggestions...

• Join a Support Group

Friends and family want to be helpful, but sometimes they just don't know how. This is when a support group – people who are experiencing the same thing you are – can be most helpful. Just hearing someone else tell their story, that they and their child lived through the same painful experience you're going through and survived to laugh and sing and enjoy another day, can give you an immeasurable boost. Your local information service or library should have lists of support groups in your area. Find someone to talk to who genuinely understands.

• Eat Well

During times of stress there is a real tendency to go the fast food or no food route. This depletes our body's ability to deal with stress and actually interferes with our brain's ability to concentrate and problem solve. Lack of good nutrition also causes physiological changes which make it difficult to sleep and decreases stamina. You don't need these added problems. If you're not up to cooking, choose fast food and restaurant foods that are good for you. (For example, veggie-packed submarines, chili beans, salad bars, lean burgers, baked potatoes, barbecued chicken, juice or milk instead of pop, yogurt or fruit ices instead of ice cream).

• Exercise

Regular exercise has enormous benefits for your mood, your body, and your well being. Do whatever you most enjoy – cycle, dance, walk, swim, aerobics, jog, ski, roller blade, weights, whatever. Don't wait until you are "in the mood" because you won't be. Do it because you must.

• Read

There are so many really good self-help books that will lift your spirits and help you get the most out of your life. Check out your local library.

• Start an Absorbing Hobby

One woman, going through a very difficult time in her life, decided that she'd always wanted to play the guitar. So she bought an inexpensive, used guitar and some books and how-to-play tapes and went at it. For several hours a day she practised and played. Those hours, when she lost herself in something other than her pain, were islands of sanity and accomplishment. Day by day, something in her life was improving. She credits her playing with keeping her sane during a time when it seemed that everything was out of her control. She came through that period of her life, sanity intact, and now plays a great guitar.

• Look for Moments of Joy

We often get so caught up in thinking that we'll be happy when ....we lose weight, or get a better job, or find a partner, or our child gets better. But if we spend our whole life waiting for the "whens" to happen, we miss all the moments of joy along the way. Be alert to the perfectly wonderful moments in your life: the early morning chatter of birds waking the world as you sip your first coffee on the back porch; the smooth touch of clean sheets when you slide your feet into a freshly-made bed; the absolutely unexpected smile of a stranger on the street; the fresh, tangy sweet juice of a perfect orange; the warmth that suffuses the soul when a small child snuggles close. Look for the moments of joy in your life. Enjoy them, collect them, and string them all together into a life that one day you'll describe as, yeah, happy.

~ Chapter Thirteen ~

FAMILY TRANSITIONS
Separation, Divorce, and Single Parenting

Will the Kids Recover?

Parents want to know if their kids will recover from separation and divorce or be scarred and emotionally damaged forever. It's a big question, but fortunately, one that we now know quite a bit about. Children can adjust to separation and divorce. How the family is structured is not the issue because children can do very, very well in single-parent or step-families. What does permanent damage, however, is the uncertainty and ongoing conflict that often continues for years after a divorce. Children are severely, permanently damaged by ongoing conflict. Fortunately, this is an area where most parents have quite a bit of control.

Single Parenting

Within the term "single parenting" there are a number of distinctly different family structures. It's worth acknowledging that single parenting is arrived at by different paths because these differing paths can significantly affect what issues the families must deal with.

For Example: A single parent who chooses artificial insemination by an anonymous donor will experience very different challenges than someone who arrives at single parenting via divorce. In the first case there truly never was and never will be a second biological parent involved in that child's life. Compared with the divorced family, this path appears to offer a family structure with blessedly few conflicts or complications. However, it also offers fewer potential family members to love and share in the care of that child.

In another example the biological father may be known, but by his or the mother's choice, he was not ever involved in the child's life. Increasingly, we are also now hearing of cases where biological mothers choose to relinquish their infants, but biological fathers assert their right to raise their babies. As well, single people of both sexes are also increasingly choosing to adopt children, another path to single parenthood. Others arrive at single parenthood because their spouse has died. In these cases there is no complicating "ex" involved, but the grief issues are significant.

When a parent arrives at single parenting by separation and divorce, the term can often be a misnomer. Although in some cases one parent definitively walks out of their children's lives, in most cases some level of involvement continues. Even if one parent has full-time custody and responsibility for the day-to-day needs of the children, the other parent, for better or worse, will always be a factor to be reckoned with. Most children do, in fact, have two involved parents.

For years these families have been referred to as "broken homes". This term is offensive. "Broken" implies something that doesn't work and that is not something anyone can generalize about. Plenty of two-parent families are dysfunctional, even abusive. Having two parents guarantees absolutely nothing. On the other side, many single parents are doing a terrific job of raising their kids. Others are not. The structure of the family does not determine the quality of the parenting; the people involved do.

This chapter has opened by identifying some of the different paths parents take to arrive at single parenthood because it's important to acknowledge that we all have different issues, different challenges to surmount; and different strengths and resources available to us. There are no

The structure of the family does not determine the quality of the parenting; the people involved do.

Another caring adult may be able to absorb some
of their grief and anger and these connections
should be encouraged.

one-size-fits-all solutions. Instead, there are lots of ideas and insights to share. Browse through the ideas that follow and think about those things that make sense to you and might work in your situation.

WHAT PARENTS NEED

In the first year following their parent's separation, children often receive less attention, affection, support, and consistent discipline. This won't come as a surprise to anyone who's been there. The sense of loss, grief, devastation, and vulnerability that most people feel when they separate and divorce can be so overwhelming that the children get lost in the pain.

You may not feel like you have the emotional resources to cope with your children's needs, but you must find them. Your children have already lost the day-to-day presence of one parent, they cannot afford to lose the other one too.

There are counsellors, support groups, and many excellent books to help you sort through your own emotions. Use them and lean on friends, family, and people like your children's coaches and teachers. If you tell them what's going on they will usually be glad to spend extra time with your kids and may be the lifeline you and your kids need. Your kids will have lots of grief and anger of their own to express and may feel they can't lay it on you. Another caring adult may be able to absorb some of that and these connections should be encouraged. As well, your son or daughter's behaviour is likely to change during the initial months after separation and their teachers and coaches need to know why. They'll usually be glad to cut your kids some slack, but they need to know.

Be good to yourself. Learn relaxation techniques, a good way to com-

People often think alcohol will make them feel better, and it may seem so in the short term, but the truth is that alcohol is a depressant.

bat both the physical and emotional effects of stress on your body. Relaxation techniques are especially useful for putting yourself to sleep, something that stress often interferes with. More than at any other time, you need your rest.

Physical exercise is helpful too as it relaxes tense muscles, increases energy levels, clears your mind, and helps you sort out problems. Pay special attention to your nutrition too during this time, it will have a major effect on how relaxed or jumpy you're feeling. Good, healthy choices will make a big difference in how much you and your children can cope with.

Go for a massage from a registered massage therapist. Many medical insurance plans pay for them and the benefits are both physical and emotional. Physically, a massage relaxes tense muscles (a source of pain, particularly headaches and neck pain) and stimulates blood flow (and consequently healing) to tissue which may have been damaged by prolonged stress. Emotionally, a massage is a wonderful way of nurturing yourself. It's an hour in your life when someone else is 100% focused on caring for you and that has inestimable benefits. Parents, particularly single parents, do not get much nurturing and particularly if your marriage has been unhappy and stressful, you are probably in a real deficit position when it comes to having your own needs met. A massage is just for you and you will feel worlds better when you walk out of there.

People often think alcohol will make them feel better, and it may seem so in the short term, but the truth is that alcohol is a depressant. If drinking becomes a regular part of your life it will bring you down and make everything much worse. Drugs as well, even commonly used drugs like marijuana, alter how we think (that's why people take them), and over time, distort reality. People who are regular users of marijuana, for example, are much more likely to commit suicide.

Separation and divorce are a process that take a long time and you will need to be patient with yourself. Don't try to do this alone; look for other adults you can talk things through with. These could be friends or family, or professionals. Ask for help from social agencies, mental health offices, family places, women's centres, support groups and other single parents. Although you shouldn't hide your feelings from your kids, don't make them your confidantes. You are an adult with adult problems; they are your children. More than at any other time, they need to believe that you are in control, that you are still capable of being the parent in your relationship. Find other adults with whom you can break down and fall apart and unload your anger and unhappiness.

> *More than at any other time, they need to believe that you are in control, that you are still capable of being the parent in your relationship.*

PARENTIFICATION: The "Too Good" Kid

Many kids appear to have great strength and there is an enormous temptation to lean on them for support. They are wonderful about taking over at home, making sure the younger ones get their homework done or have their bath. They put dinner on, unload the dryer, and press your shirt when you're running late. They're great about running interference for you too; answering the phone and telling people you're not available. These great kids are there when your ex is late with the support cheque and you explode in anger. They rub your feet and shush the little ones so you don't have to deal with them. Quite simply, you don't know what you'd do without them.

It's called "parentification" and it is so easy for any parent, overwhelmed by responsibilities, grief, illness or problems, to let their child slip into this role. The parent doesn't even notice it happening. Some kids are just so great, they make it so easy. But the thing is, in supporting our needs, they suppress their own. They push their own fear, anger, concern and worries into the background so they can keep us strong.

In the short run, this role reversal, where the kid takes on a parenting

But, in supporting our needs, they suppress their own.

role, is gratifying for both parent and child. Adults have their needs taken care of while the child enjoys the power and importance of their role as mini-parent.

Longer term however, it really mixes a kid up. They grow up being overly-responsible for everyone, guilty about saying no, unable to set limits on how others use them, unable to relinquish control to others, and threatened by intimacy because they've never learned to receive or been taken care of themselves. These kids, who spend their youth as mini-adults, actually have great difficulty becoming emotionally healthy adults.

Identifying Parentification

Parentification is much more than asking your children to help out, it's permitting them to turn themselves into another parent. The following questions will help show that difference.

1. Are you in charge of the household and is everyone clear on that?

2. It's good for everyone in the family to have responsibilities and these should genuinely contribute to the family's wellbeing, but are these responsibilities so great that they are cutting into your children's schoolwork, social activities, sports, or clubs?

3. Do you have adult confidantes or are you depending on your son or daughter for emotional support?

4. Do you ask your son or daughter to screen telephone calls or visitors so that you don't have to deal with difficult people or creditors? The parent, not the child, needs to be the family gatekeeper.

5. Do you describe your son or daughter as your lifeline? Do other people comment on how perfect they are?

These "too good to be true" kids show up, not just in single-parent households, but in any situations where parents are overwhelmed by factors like chronic illness, alcoholism, disabilities, the needs of other children, a frequently absent partner, violence, and so on. We all need to be on the alert for a pattern of relying too heavily on the child that is always willing to be there for us.

Kids are absolutely shameless about listening at doors ... they probably already know far more than you'd expect.

WHAT KIDS NEED

Sometimes, parents see separation and divorce as a second chance for themselves. Teens don't usually see it that way. To them, separation or divorce is the loss of their family and while you might be happy to see the last of your spouse, teens do not usually feel that way about losing their other parent. For them it's a very real, major loss in their life and one they need to grieve.

Teens, especially, are at a point in their lives where they need to be assuming control. Instead, their parents' separation presents them with a major change over which they are completely powerless. To make things worse, the separation often means some significant lifestyle changes: less money to pay for team sports, clothes, movies, and holidays; and frequently, a move to a new house and school. This is generally the exact opposite of what teens need at this stage in their lives.

Telling the Kids

To begin with, talk to them (both parents together, if possible) about the separation or divorce. They need to know what is happening and how it will affect them. Honestly, but without the gory details, tell them why you are separating or divorcing. Teens are absolutely shameless about listening at doors and so on, so don't be surprised if they don't already know far, far, more than you'd expect.

They will want to know what the chances are of you getting back together, so be honest about this. They'll need as much reassurance as possible about the practicalities of how they'll be living.

> *For Example:*
> *When will they be able to see the non-resident parent?*
> *Where will they live?*
> *Will they have to change schools?*
> *Can they keep playing on the same hockey team?*
> *Is there going to be less money and what will that mean?*

Be as honest and accurate about all this as you can, cautioning them that there are some things you just won't know right away. Assure them that they'll be the first to know when things change or become clearer (and make sure they are).

Encourage discussion but realize that kids often need time to digest information. Even if they've suspected what's going on, the reality of it will hit them very hard. Assure them that you are willing to talk about it as often, and whenever, they need to. Be aware that they may spend days, weeks or even months ruminating on something, then need to re-visit a discussion you thought was long over.

Kids all behave differently. Some will express their emotions overtly and openly, while others will express it through their behaviour. Encourage them to talk to you, to their other parent, to other adults, and their friends. Be more tolerant of the expression of angry emotions than you might usually be, but make a clear distinction between angry feelings and behaviour. Angry feelings are okay and normal for the circumstances, expressing that anger by trashing the house or beating up someone isn't. Help them find healthy outlets for their emotions like: running,

Teens, especially, are at a point in their lives where they need to be assuming control. Instead, their parents' separation presents them with a major change over which they are completely powerless.

working out, biking, working with clay, writing a journal, playing drums, or talking to others.

If their other parent is choosing not to see them, help your kids understand that this says nothing about their value, but only shows how screwed up the other parent is right now. In this case, especially, take your son or daughter's coaches and teachers into your confidence and tell them what is happening. Your children's self esteem will really be battered by their other parent's indifference and having other adults show them that they're valued will help.

Getting Your Lives Back on Track

Try to get your lives back into a routine as quickly as possible. Kids need the security of knowing what comes next and re-establishing routines and schedules will go a long way in this regard. Hold regular family council meetings to help you decide, together, how to realign responsibilities and choose your priorities as a family.

Together, talk about how you'll set priorities for spending money. It is likely that family income has been significantly reduced and your home life will be less stressful if everyone has had a voice in deciding which financial commitments to keep and which they can live without. You are still the parent and the final decision may need to be yours, but you may be surprised by how creative your kids are. They will suggest solutions that you would never have thought of. At the least, having this discussion and taking their ideas into account will make it much easier for everyone to understand why they cannot have everything they want, when they want it.

Visualize your family as being in a boat with each member on an oar. If you can all agree on where you're going, then row in the same direction, your boat will move steadily toward a common objective. However, if everyone is rowing in a different direction, the boat will do donuts in the marina. You'll go nowhere and may well capsize. Family council meetings help families set their oars in the same direction.

Discipline

Discipline may become more difficult with teens after separation and divorce. Teens are likely to be angry and insecure. They use their behaviour to try limits and boundaries, testing to see whether their parent is going to remain reliably in control or not.

After the stress of separation, parents can be insecure themselves. They are vulnerable to their children's approval and afraid of rejection. Quite often, the parent is afraid that their son or daughter may decide they'd rather live with the other parent. Children very quickly catch on, playing one parent against the other. They will use this fear to manipulate their parents, push limits and ignore rules. A parent who was formerly a firm disciplinarian begins to plead with their kids to behave. This turns into a really bad scene for everyone.

While you do need to cut kids a little slack during the immediate post-separation period, they also need the security of a parent who is in charge. As a family, examine whether the house rules need modification now that you're living in different circumstances, but make sure your kids know where you stand and what you will tolerate.

Leaving home or running away is an option that kids from all kinds of families have fantasies about. The difference with kids from separated or divorced families is that they believe they have a real alternative – the other parent.

The fear that kids will leave and go live with their other parent is a real one that needs to be faced.

Even those teens whose other parent has abandoned the family and not been seen for years will maintain this fantasy as a viable option.

The fear that kids will leave and go live with their other parent is a real one that needs to be faced. Realistic or not, many kids from separated or divorced families believe they have this alternative and if allowed, use it to blackmail their parent.

The question is, will the parent let it happen?

If the cost of keeping a teen at home is constant turmoil, disrespect, and behaviour so obnoxious that everyone is miserable, is it worth it?

Would it be better to state limits, declare what behaviour is acceptable or unacceptable and tell the teen that if they cannot comply, the other parent will be called and asked for a meeting to discuss a change in the teen's living arrangements?

> *If the cost of keeping a teen at home is constant turmoil, disrespect, and behaviour so obnoxious that everyone is miserable, is it worth it?*

In two-parent homes it is normal, at any given time, for one parent to relate to or "handle" one teen better than the other parent. This may be true for six months or a year, then change so that the teen relates better to the other parent. This is normal family life. The only difference in single-parent families is that spending more time with another parent may mean a change (often temporary) in where the teen lives.

Assuming their other parent is a decent human being, having your teen move in with them can have some real benefits to your relationship with your teen. Without the stress of ongoing, daily conflict and the constant pressure of the teen's threat to move, you will each have some important breathing space. It will give you both time to re-think your relationship and, hopefully, rediscover what you really like and enjoy about each other.

Very often too, teens come to a point in their development where they need to spend time with the other parent. Each parent gives very different things to their children and to complete their development they may need to spend a lot more time with the parent they've been missing. To do that, they may need to change where they live.

> *For Example: Sarah's parents have been divorced since she was five. She lives with her mother and because her father lives 2,000 miles away, only sees him at Christmas and for a month in the summer. She's now fifteen and finds herself looking enviously at her friend's fathers. She misses her Dad so much, sometimes she feels physical pain in her chest. She doesn't understand this father-hunger. After all, in her memory, he's never been part of her daily life so why should she be missing him so much right now?*

The one positive thing about separation or divorce could be an end to the fighting. Unfortunately, for many, the warfare just escalates.

If Sarah's mother acknowledges Sarah's need to spend time with her father and gives her blessing to Sarah moving across the country, it will no doubt be the most difficult thing she's ever done. Perhaps a compromise could be reached where Sarah spends the whole summer with her father. Or maybe father and daughter could both hook up to e-mail and in that way, be much more accessible to each other. What is important, is that Sarah's need for more fathering be acknowledged and dealt with.

Parenting is about doing what is in the best interests of a child and, very often, that calls for great sacrifice on the part of the parent. The reward, however, is a healthy, happy young adult and nothing is more satisfying.

THE PARENT-TO-PARENT RELATIONSHIP

Researchers say that kids from divorced families appear to have more problems and lower levels of well-being than kids from intact families. But the research also shows that these problems are not caused by the divorce itself, or from living in a single-parent family. These long-term problems are the result of being exposed to ongoing parental conflict.

From the teen's point of view, the one positive thing about separation or divorce could be that it means an end to the fighting. Unfortunately, for many, the warfare just escalates. Now, on top of all the other things they used to fight about, their parents battle over support cheques, visitation schedules, how late he let the kids stay up, how she had a man overnight, who is going to pay for the orthodontist, who'll take the kids to soccer, and where will they spend Christmas. It goes on and on and what's worse, their battles are now clearly "child-centred". This means their children now see themselves as the direct cause of their parent's fighting. This places an unbearable burden on children's shoulders. Not only was the marriage a failure, so is the divorce.

Make no mistake, prolonged conflict will seriously, permanently, damage your children.

> *Your children are depending on you to do what is best for them and in almost all cases, they need a reliable and close relationship with both parents.*

Make it a Working Relationship

If you can't establish a good relationship with your ex-spouse, make it a workable, business-like one. Yes, this may call for you to bite your tongue till it bleeds, but you have to do it. Your children are depending on you to do what is best for them and in almost all cases, they need a reliable and close relationship with both parents.

Your relationship with your ex-spouse will continue for many, many years into the future. Not only will you always both be parents of the same children, but at some time in the future you will probably be grandparents of the same grandchildren. It is to your advantage to try and establish a workable relationship with this person.

A good technique for doing this is to think of your relationship with this person as having two parts. There is the spousal relationship which caused and probably continues to cause you pain, anguish and frustration. Separate this from the relationship you have as parents of the same children. In your mind and in how you deal with your ex-spouse, keep these relationships separate and do not allow the issues to get mixed up together. Tell your ex-spouse what you are doing and ask him or her, for the sake of the kids you both love, to do the same. Think about the characteristics of good business relationships (scheduled meetings, agendas, written agreements, no emotional involvement) and use that kind of relationship as your model for your parent-to-parent behaviour.

Someplace neutral, like a restaurant, sit down with your children's other parent and formalize your parenting roles and responsibilities. Write down the decisions you make. Here are some issues you might want to talk about:

Parent to Parent

1. How will you communicate?
2. What decisions will you share?
3. Will each of you commit to encouraging a relationship between the kids and the other parent?
4. When will the kids be with each of you?
5. What will happen around vacations?
6. What if one of you is supposed to have the kids but can't. What kind of notice is appropriate?
7. School holidays?
8. Can you agree on common ground rules for basic issues like curfews, homework, dating, and so on?
9. How will the kids maintain their relationships with cousins and grandparents?
10. Who will attend teacher conferences at the school?
11. How will the kids be supported and where will they live?
12. Who will pay for and make decisions around medical, dental, childcare, college?
13. How will disputes be settled?

If your relationship is still too volatile to allow you to discuss these things calmly, book an appointment with a mediator. These professionals have a great deal of success in helping couples come to agreement on issues around children because in most cases, what both parents really want, down deep in their hearts, is what is best for their kids. A mediator can help you both work from that premise, instead of from the hurt and anger that is still on the surface and stage managing your behaviour towards each other.

Kids are Creative

Your kids will be very inventive about getting you back together and that may take the form of getting into trouble. They quickly figure out that if they get into serious enough trouble you will respond as a team and they will have reunited you, even if it's only at the police station. Let them know you're wise to them. Point out that nothing they do will change your decision to separate or divorce. It was an adult decision that was made by their parents. They cannot affect it.

If kids can't have what they really want – their family back together – they'll go after the next best thing – stuff. By playing one parent against the other they can earn all kinds of perks, prizes, and privileges. This is where that working relationship with your ex-spouse comes in. You need to talk to each other. If you can agree not to outbid each other, your children will be much more pleasant human beings and you'll have done them an enormous favour.

Kids quickly figure out that if they get into serious enough trouble you will respond as a team and they will have reunited you, even if it's only at the police station.

If possible, agree with your children's other parent on the ground rules of daily life for your kids. If it's not possible for you to agree, don't worry too much about it. Stay consistent in your own home and relationship with your kids. They are accustomed to dealing with the different rules and expectations of many people (teachers, coaches, work supervisors) and will adjust to different expectations between parents too.

"Ex" tended Family

Remember that even though your spouse and his parents and siblings are "ex" to you, they are not "ex" to your kids. These are still their grandparents, aunts, uncles, and cousins. They need to have these people in their lives. Make it clear (perhaps by a letter to your in-laws) that you do not want to stand in the way of these relationships. If these people are denigrating you to your children, make it clear this must stop for the sake of the kids. Like your relationship with your ex-spouse, try to maintain, at minimum, a civil relationship with these people. The continuity of relationships and traditions and routines are important stabilizing factors in your children's lives.

Kids are very loyal and may believe that if they allow themselves to feel happy about going off for the weekend with their other parent, they are being disloyal to you.

BETWEEN HOUSES

Having the kids spend time with their other parent is not a reward for support payments. They really need to spend time with you both. If support cheques are not arriving as they should, try to separate your anger over this from your children's need to spend time with the other parent. Deal with the support cheque problem in private, away from the kids.

Custodial parents often worry that the other parent is spoiling the kids – letting them stay up too late and feeding them junk food. Try to ignore your resentment about this. Your children really need to spend time with this parent and whatever the effects of late nights and shabby nutrition might be, they are nothing compared to the loss children feel when they are deprived of one parent. Furthermore, they don't need you grumbling and denigrating their other parent every time they return home or they will become stressed out and apprehensive about returning to your home.

However much they might need to spend time with the other parent, moving between homes reminds them that their family is no longer together. The act of packing their bags and changing houses makes this reality jump up and smack them in the face. This realization can make them act out when they first return to your home. Parents often blame this behaviour on the "other" parent, assuming that since they've just come from the "other" house, it must be that parents fault. It usually isn't. Give your kids some space to level out and make some peace with this when they first return home. While acting out emotions by being destructive or hurting other people is not acceptable, feeling those emotions is necessary.

You will help them make this transition between homes if you can

Learn to anticipate those weekends and holidays when the kids are away as times to concentrate on yourself and your own interests.

genuinely encourage them to go off with the other parent and have a good time. Kids are very loyal and may believe that if they allow themselves to feel happy about going off for the weekend with their other parent, they are being disloyal to you. This will deter them from getting on with their lives and adjusting to the separation or divorce. Let them know it's okay to love you both.

Separation and divorce are never what any of us dreams of when we think of the future. But it happens, and when it does, parents and children have to accept it and move on with their lives, finding happiness within the context of reality. The house will seem very empty when they are away, so find new activities and people to fill those empty hours. Learn to anticipate those weekends and holidays when the kids are away as times to concentrate on yourself and your own interests. The kids will pick up on your contentment and feel much less strain about moving between homes.

If your teen wants to talk about their other parent, listen, but don't pump them for information. This is an enormous temptation, but really try not to. Similarly, try not to send "messages" with your kids. Pick up the phone and settle issues with the other parent, yourself, in private.

It goes without saying that criticizing the other parent is very destructive to your kids, but it's so important I'll say it anyway. Being critical of the other parent sets things up as an either/or situation. It puts kids in the position of loving one parent or the other, of being loyal to one parent or the other parent, of having a good time with one parent or the other, etc. This is an intolerable stress for kids and will permanently damage them.

You may have very strong and negative emotions about your ex-spouse for a long time. Find a friend, another single-parent, a family-member, a support group or a counsellor to vent these feelings with, but leave your kids out of it. They need to love you both.

WHEN THE KIDS DON'T LIVE WITH YOU FULL-TIME

Parents who do not have full-time custody of their kids often believe that they have lost their role as a parent. This is absolutely not true. You are still a parent and you will always be a parent. Nothing, not even your ex-spouse's remarriage will change the fact you are your children's mother or father and they need you.

What you may have to be is much more thoughtful and creative about how you parent. Start by thinking about how you view your kids "visitation". Are they really a visitor to your home? Is this how you want them to feel?

Make a place for them that is theirs alone. Best, of course, is a room of their own that no one but they have access to. If this is not possible, how about a cot and a chest of drawers (with a locking drawer for their private things) that no one but they use? Try to avoid having them sleep on a pull-out couch while they live out of a suitcase, because this truly puts them in the position of being a temporary visitor. They are in your life for good, so make a place for them in your home, that is theirs alone.

Keep things just for them: toothbrush, hairbrush, favourite shampoo, and so on. Take them shopping for at least a few clothes (like pyjamas) they can leave at your home. Stock your cupboards with the cereal they eat, the canned ravioli they like, the juice they prefer. Expect them to clean up after themselves and share in the chores of family life. Make your home their home.

When your children are only with you for short periods of time there is a temptation to ignore discipline. Just as custodial parents worry that if there is conflict the kids will move out, non-custodial parents worry that their kids won't come at all. Letting these worries dictate how you parent is a real disservice to your kids. Remember that you are their parent and that means you have a responsibility to parent them in ways that will help them develop into healthy, caring adults. Be clear about your expectations and consistent in enforcing house rules. At the same time, don't waste your time together nit-picking about things that aren't your responsibility anymore.

For example: Mary Ann's fifteen-year-old son Nick spends one week-end a month and three weeks in the summer with her. A major source of conflict between them has always been Nick's choice of

There are going to be times when they arrive at your house, throw their bag in the door and revolve right back out.

clothing and hairstyle. He favours grungy old clothes from the Goodwill and recently had his eyebrow pierced. She's furious that her ex-husband would permit this and has demanded that Nick remove the ring when he's with her. He frequently "forgets" and they spend too much of their time together arguing about this. If Mary Ann could accept that day-to-day supervision of Nick is no longer her responsibility, the conflict that is so much a part of their time together would largely disappear. She would probably find that in a more relaxed, enjoyable relationship she would have much more influence over Nick.

Your time together is going to feel much more contrived than it was when you lived together full time. Accept this and look for activities and interests that you both genuinely enjoy and can look forward to sharing: work out together, play cards, be movie critics, bike, play music together, become garage sale junkies, go backpacking, cook together, teach her how to drive, join a rock climbing gym, play chess, take a clay class together, play tennis, go fishing, learn how to kayak, play the stock market, turn into art critics, play video games, or take a photography course together and set up a darkroom. The important thing is that these interests be something that you both genuinely enjoy and look forward to.

Realize, though, that teens are self-centred. This is the normal state of being for kids at this stage of development. There are going to be times when they arrive at your house, throw their bag in the door and revolve right back out with a hurried, "Hi! Glad to see ya. Going to the movies with Cathy, back by 11, don't worry, see ya then!" You may have been eagerly anticipating their visit and be deeply hurt by this. Try not to be. It's not personal. If anything, it probably indicates a comfort level with you that should make you feel good. They're treating you like they would if you still lived together all the time.

There will be other times when they won't want to come over because they've got plans with their friends. This is normal too and although deeply disappointing, try to ride it out without making your kids feel guilty. They will mature into wonderful adults who are thoughtful about your feelings – eventually. The most important people in a teen's life are his or her parents. Unfortunately that doesn't usually translate into us being the person they want to hang out with on Saturday night. If you find that your teen is regularly cancelling weekend visits, re-think the visitation schedule. Flexibility is the key to a good relationship with teens. Parents are simply not their priority at this time in their life and that is the way it is supposed to be! Perhaps dinner several times a week or

The most important people in a teen's life are his or her parents ...that doesn't translate into us being the person they want to hang out with on Saturday night.

*Designate a new day the "Un-Birthday"
and celebrate with pizza .*

breakfast on Sunday would be more compatible and more satisfying for both of you at this time in their lives.

As your kids grow up your relationship with them will evolve and your time together will change. It's normal for a five-year-old to spend a whole weekend with his parent. It's not normal for a fifteen-year-old. This is true whether your teen lives with you full time or sees you periodically.

Maintaining the Connection

Make yourself accessible to your teens on their terms. Can they call you when they need you? Do they have your work number? If you are spending a lot of time with a new relationship can they reach you there too? If you live long distance and can afford it, think about getting them a calling card.

Sending postcards, notes, and letters is also a great way to communicate with kids. Telling them how you feel in writing gives them something they can look at again and again. Especially in those first weeks after separation they may well be too shell shocked to remember what you tell them verbally and reassuring them in writing that you will always love them and be there for them, gives them something they can hang onto.

Everyone loves old-fashioned mail, so clip cartoons, news stories, magazine articles, pictures, jokes, postcards, and so on that you think might interest them and pop them in the mail. It might sound hokey, but it's concrete evidence that you are thinking about them, that they are important to you and they need that reassurance, over and over again. Just don't expect them to write back. Writing a letter would be too much like school work for most teens. Give them a handful of pre-addressed and stamped envelopes, because miracles do happen, but be realistic and send mail because you love them and want them to know it.

Teens today are much more likely to use e-mail and because it is such a spontaneous style of communication, it can be an excellent window into their lives. If one or both of you don't have an internet connection at home, don't let it stop you. Go to your local library and learn how to set up a private, no cost e-mail address for each of you. These days, lack of funds does not keep anyone from utilizing the benefits of the internet.

Photos are memories we can touch, so when you're together take lots of pictures. Blow them up, frame them, stick them on the fridge and mail copies to your kids. Like a letter, it's something they can hold onto when you're not there.

Holiday Heartaches

Who gets the kids for the holidays is often such a source of stress that everyone, especially the kids, start to dread them. Try to remember that just because somebody somewhere, a long, long time ago designated that a particular holiday should be celebrated on a particular day, doesn't mean that's the only time families can enjoy each other. If you can't be together on Christmas Day, start a new tradition of spending Christmas Eve, or Boxing Day, or New Year's Day together. If Easter won't work, make St. Patrick's Day a big deal. If you'll be apart on one of your birthdays designate a new day the "Un-Birthday" and celebrate with pizza instead of cake. Be creative. Concentrate on what is possible and make your lives the best and happiest they can be.

Trying Harder

Establishing that working parental relationship with your children's other parent will enable you to co-operate for the benefit of your kids. This will also help you have more informal access to your kids. Even though it might not be your "day" or "weekend" to have custody of your kids, offer to share the driving to hockey, dance, soccer, piano, ringette, practices. The car is a great place for teens and parents to have sensitive conversations. Encourage your ex-spouse to share the "work" of parenthood, like chauffeur duties, with you. Make it clear that you want to stay involved, not just to have fun with your children, but to share the work of parenting as well.

Ask your teens to give you a schedule of their games, recitals, or presentations, and be there for them. They will be looking for you. Better yet, offer to be a coach or timekeeper or team manager or ticket taker or fundraiser. You are their parent and you have both a right and responsibility to be part of their lives in significant ways.

You may not be able to help them with their day-to-day schoolwork, but ask them about their longer-term projects and papers. Even if you live at some distance you can help them by looking for articles and research items that are pertinent to their projects.

The point is, you are still their parent and always will be. Just knowing that you love them and are still in there pitching as a parent has a profound effect on the well-being of your kids. Sometimes, non-custodial parents feel they are being pushed out of the way (particularly when a stepparent is now part of the custodial home) and this may be so. Don't let your frustration or jealousy or anger at your ex-spouse get in the way of your relationship with your teen. They need you. There may well be other people in their lives who play significant roles and frankly, the more caring adults a teen has around them the better, but do not ever be mistaken, you cannot be replaced.

You may have to do your parenting under different circumstances than you'd planned, but you are the only father or mother your teen will ever have. That role is yours alone and it carries with it both significant responsibility and profound joy.

~ Chapter Fourteen ~

FAMILY TRANSITIONS
Building a Stepfamily

It takes effort to make a stepfamily work, but there are many families who will tell you it's worth it. This chapter takes a realistic look at the challenges and offers ideas for building a happy life together.

THE COUPLE: The Foundation of the Family

How well a stepfamily is going to function is often determined by how secure and supportive the couple are of each other. In the first throes of romance, most couples are adamant about the strength of their relationship. But frankly, lust and love wear thin real fast in a household of hostile teenagers.

Unlike a first marriage, there is no two to three year honeymoon period during which the couple, alone, strengthen the bond between them and adjust to living with each other. First time couples usually

> *Lust and love wear thin real fast in a household of hostile teenagers.*

have several years to fill a memory bank with wonderful, warm, intimate experiences. This "bank" of good feeling is what couples normally draw on during the periods in a marriage when life is tense and stressful.

A second marriage, with teens involved, catapults the new couple into the middle of many complex relationships that require huge quantities of attention and energy. Finding time for their private, couple relationship,

Taking a course together gives couples a non-threatening environment in which to discuss parenting styles.

is difficult. It's necessary, however, because the couple relationship is the foundation on which the family is built and it needs to be both strong and flexible. Knowing that there are going to be extra challenges in forming a stepfamily, a couple needs to be proactive about reinforcing their relationship.

Marriage: A Learning Experience

Marriage or remarriage preparation and education courses explore issues like: how to communicate so that you really hear and understand each other; how to resolve conflicts so everyone wins; how your families of origin affect what your expectations of each other and your family are; and how to set goals as a couple. A good couple education course is an important investment in the strength and resiliency of a relationship and the family that depends on that relationship.

Becoming skilful communicators is particularly important to second marriages because they are so much more complex. When we think of all the relationships involved: his kids; her kids; those kids' biological parents; extended families that include in-laws, out-laws, and long-term friends; maternal and paternal groups on both sides; the mind boggles. The opportunities for miscues and misunderstandings are numerous; especially when, with kids involved, the ex-spouse (even if they are dead) is never, ever completely out of the picture.

Couples should also consider taking a parenting course together. They may both feel that they are excellent parents and don't need such a course, but it's likely that their parenting styles have some differences. Taking a course together gives couples a non-threatening environment in which to discuss parenting styles, consider new ideas, and work out a mutual plan for their joint family. It's very important for couples to have these discussions and work out their parenting differences away from the kids. They need to present a well-thought-out, united, front and they can't do that if they haven't even discussed what their individual positions are. While issues are still in the realm of the theoretical, parents need to decide how issues like alcohol and drug use, curfews, chores, allowance, and so on will be handled. Once the issues are personal, and emotions are involved, it will be much more difficult to achieve consensus.

The new family deserves a home where everyone starts on an equal footing; a home where space is divided up according to need, not prior claim, and where furnishings have been chosen from both families' collections.

NEW FAMILY - NEW HOME

An important question for the new couple to resolve, is the matter of where the family will live. A new space, neutral territory for everyone, is usually best. Otherwise, whomever moves into the established home will feel like an intruder, both spatially and emotionally. Spatially, the family whose original home it is, will have long ago divided up the house and claimed territory. It is very difficult, especially for teens, to give up rooms that have been theirs for years. They will resent it. There is also the issue of furnishings; a home that's been lived in for years will have all the furniture, pictures, and dishes it needs. Where do the belongings of the incoming family go? If they have to abandon the things that for them, make a house home, they'll be both resentful and have difficulty feeling that the new space is their home.

Furthermore, homes hold the emotional ghosts of those who have lived there before. The whole house, and everything in it, will remind the newcomers that someone else was the husband or wife before them. Jealousy is a powerful human emotion and it poisons relationships.

The new family deserves a home where everyone starts on an equal footing; a home where space is divided up according to need, not prior claim, and where furnishings have been chosen from both families' collections. As well, in a home that is new to each member of the family, everyone can participate in renovating and decorating, taking ownership for the new place and truly making it their home.

WON'T THE KIDS LOVE HAVING A NEW ......?

Realize that stepfamilies are born of loss. First the kids lost their family as they knew it, and the daily presence of one parent. Now, they are losing a large part of their custodial parent's attention as he or she falls in love and spends increasing amounts of time with their new lover. From the children's point of view, remarriage is not usually the gain of an additional parent, it is a further loss of the one they live with.

What usually happens, after separation and divorce, is that the single parent and children meld together into a solid, supportive unit. The kids take over some of the duties of the absent parent and the custodial parent spends more time with the kids. New rituals are created: Friday night videos, Saturday night card games, Sunday morning pancakes, and so on. The family learns new ways of getting the business of living taken care of: one child assumes responsibility for making lunches; another takes over yardwork; Dad now does laundry; or Mom rakes leaves. There is a realignment of both chores and social activities and the longer the single-parent family exists, the more entrenched these new responsibilities and rituals become. In single-parent families where a second parent has never been involved, the exclusivity of the parent/child(ren) relationship may be even stronger.

Family Togetherness: Not For Teens

Young children, who are developmentally at a stage where they want family "togetherness", may welcome a stepparent who has taken the time to befriend them, but teens are in an altogether different developmental stage.

From their point of view, there isn't usually room in the family for another adult. This has nothing to do with whether they do or do not like the person, they simply don't want another person, a stranger, living in their house and intruding on the tight relationship they have with their parent. Adults choose to live in stepfamilies, adolescents do not usually want a stepfamily.

The make or break issue is whether the
teen believes that they've been displaced
by the stepparent.

Displacement: A Major Cause of Problems

Research into what influences the wellbeing of teens in stepfamilies shows very clearly that the make or break issue is whether the teen believes that they've been displaced by the stepparent. While it is inevitable that the teen is going to feel some displacement, it is important that the parent/child relationship be intruded upon as little as possible.

New stepparents should be cautious about disrupting established routines. They should not take over a chore like yardwork or making lunches because they assume the stepchild will be delighted to give up this work. Over time, each member of the family has pitched in to ensure the survival of the family unit and teens will probably see these good intentions as an attempt to displace them.

The biological parent should try to maintain as many of the single-parent rituals as possible with their children. While the new stepparent could be incorporated into some of them, the biological parent must preserve time to continue activities and interests alone with their children. The more secure the children feel about continuing to receive their parent's love and attention, the more open they are likely to become to accepting their parent's new partner.

Integrate Slowly

Many people come into the stepfamily relationship with fantasies about how wonderful it will be to parent and how everyone will be one big happy family. But developmentally, teens are into separation, not attachment. They can't get into attachment just because the stepparent wants it so. If the stepparent barges into the relationship determined to parent and is unwilling to see their role differently, there are bound to be major conflicts. Most children already have both a mother and a father (even if one parent is dead) and teens, particularly, do not usually want another parent.

Among counsellors who work with stepfamilies, there is a rule of thumb that it will take a child as long as they are old (at the transition to stepfamily) to accept a new person in the parental role. This means a fifteen-year-old will take fifteen years to accept the new stepparent as a parent. It is unlikely, therefor, that a teen will ever accept a stepparent in the parental role. This may be hard for the stepparent to accept, but they will come to much heartache if they insist on pushing for a role that is not theirs.

Stepfamilies that are formed when the children are teens tend to work best when the stepparent integrates into the family in a less-threatening role such as: friend, mentor, aunt, uncle, or coach. They need to move into the family in a low-key way, letting their relationship with the children evolve naturally.

It may be money well spent for a family to invest in a few sessions with a counsellor who specializes in stepfamilies. As a family, they need to explore what kind of role the new stepparent could take and how they would all like the new family to evolve. When they understand that the new stepparent is coming into the family as an *added resource*, not as a replacement for their other parent, the transition to a new family can be much easier.

Whether or not the adults ever grow to like each other is irrelevant. What is important is that they develop a relationship that permits them to take care of whatever business there is between them.

A stepparent also needs to be respectful of the children's relationship with their other biological parent (dead or alive). The kids will have pictures and mementoes in their rooms and will probably talk about this parent. The absent parent may be held up as a paragon of perfection and the stepparent compared unfavourably. There will be phone calls and visits and a need for that other parent to be present at family events like bar mitzvahs, graduations, and weddings, never mind all the day-to-day events like playoffs, recitals, and school conferences. This may not be easy for the stepparent, but kids genuinely need to maintain a relationship with their other parent. Since this person will be a part of their life for many, many years to come, it might be helpful for stepparents to think of this other parent in terms of a business relationship. Whether or not the adults ever grow to like each other is irrelevant. What is important is that they develop a relationship that permits them to take care of whatever business there is between them (like exchanging information about the children's schedules or medication) in a business-like manner that is not hurtful to either themselves or the children. No one wins when stepparents and parents line up against each other.

SIBLINGS: The Spice of Family Life

It's important that each member of the family, whether they all live together full time or not, feel they are genuinely part of the family. Major family decisions that are discussed at family meetings should be held over for a time when each member of the family can be there, or at least present on a speaker phone.

In family council meetings, the family can plan activities that everyone can do together, but togetherness shouldn't be forced. Reluctant teens will spoil the day for everyone and the whole purpose of sharing a good time together will be lost. The family event should proceed with those who genuinely want to participate and enjoy themselves. Later, talk about the great time everyone had is more likely to entice the reluctant teen to participate in a future activity, than forcing them to go when they're being stubborn.

It's quite possible that all the new stepsiblings won't like each other. After all, biological siblings often don't like each other, at least for periods of time. If one mixes in the fact that stepsiblings have been thrust into a family structure they probably don't want, and are feeling resentful about all kinds of things, it is likely that there will be conflict between the stepsiblings.

Parents cannot demand that siblings like each other. All that can reasonably be expected is that they be respectful of each other and their parents. They need time for their relationships with each other to evolve. In the meantime, the adults can model good communication and conflict resolution techniques as well as avoiding the inequities (like uneven responsibilities and spending money) and hindrances (like having one kid move into the other's room) that create more conflict.

If the new family has a fresh start in a home that is neutral to everyone, the space can be divided according to needs.

A Place of Their Own

Each of the kids need to be on an equal footing and this also needs to be expressed in terms of where they bunk and keep their personal belongings. As discussed in the chapter on separation and divorce, the "visiting" kids need a place of their own and their "visits" should not displace their stepsibling. If the resident teen is forced to make major accommodations every time their stepsibling comes over, it will lead to resentment. Kids are very territorial and the newcomer will be made to feel like an interloper while the resident sib will feel that their space has been invaded.

If the new family has a fresh start in a home that is neutral to everyone, the space can be divided according to needs. Exact equality may not be the way to go if there is limited space and one sibling only lives there for three-to-four weeks of the year, but if the whole family sits down together and works at an equitable (according to each person's needs, rather than mathematically equal) division of space, there is much more likely to be a spirit of willingness and cooperation.

For Example: Susan and her stepsister Lindy have to share a room. However, since Lindy only lives in the house one weekend a month and three weeks during the summer, it doesn't make sense for them to split the room down the middle. In a family meeting, the girls decided that bunk beds would work for them, with Lindy having the upper bunk. Lindy feels strongly that she doesn't want anyone else sleeping in her bed and Susan agreed to respect this. If she has friends sleep over, they'll sleep on a foamy on the floor. Lindy also asked for a chest of drawers of her own with a locking drawer and assurance that when she isn't there, Susan won't use her clothes. One wall of the shared room is reserved for Lindy's posters and stuff, as well as a section of the closet. Both girls are happy with this arrangement. Susan has exclusive possession of the room most of the time, but Lindy feels at home among her own things when she comes; not an interloper or visitor.

Consistent Ground Rules

It's important that all the kids in one family, even if some of them are only in the home part time, have consistent ground rules.

For Example: Jordan and Kathy, who live in the home full time, are expected to load and unload the dishwasher, make their beds, fold laundry and clean one bathroom every week. Their stepsibling, Linnea, comes to be with her father every second weekend. Linnea is not expected to do anything and, in fact, does not even make her bed, which totally infuriates Kathy who shares a room with her. Before long, Jordan and Kathy, who never before objected to doing chores were refusing to do anything. "Why should we," they said, "Linnea doesn't have to."

The idea that someone would love both their biological children and their stepchildren the same is ludicrous.

Time Alone With Bio Parent

Teens need to spend time alone with their biological parent and this should be encouraged within the family. Care should be taken that there aren't obvious financial inequities around this (for example, one parent taking "her" kids to Disneyland for a week, while the other one takes "his" kids to the discount movie).

The idea that someone would love both their biological children and their stepchildren the same is ludicrous. A parent has a bond with their own biological children that is deep and special and needs to be honoured. Living in a stepfamily is not something most teens would choose for themselves, and remarriage has meant that they've lost a lot of their parent's attention. The biological parent they live with needs to set aside exclusive time for them alone.

Discipline

This is the area where stepparents and teens come into the greatest conflict because teens are very unlikely to grant a new steppparent the moral authority necessary to be a disciplinarian. Insisting on doing so, on coming into a family of teenagers, will only lead to ongoing and distructive power struggles between the stepparent and teen.

Stepparents need to think of themselves as a consultant to the biological parent. Both parents talk things out together and problem solve together, but it is the biological parent who is responsible for setting and enforcing the rules with their own kids. The stepparent needs to be able to live with whatever they decide, but the biological parent has to be the one front and centre with their own kids.

Many times, problems that get blamed on the kids actually result from a conflict in values between the adults.

For Example: Anita and her two sons have been living a hectic, but for them, happy lifestyle. Anita works fulltime and volunteers at the Women's Shelter several evenings a week. Her boys play hockey, so she spends several evenings and time on the weekends, cheering them on. The boys also spend hours and hours each week practising with their basement rock band and both boys pride themselves on being good students. The last thing any of them, including Anita, worry about, is the housework. Their house shows it – chaotic, but happy.

When Ken married Anita he thought she would slow down some. It had been difficult finding enough time to date, let alone fall in love. Now that they were married he planned to enjoy a more peaceful lifestyle. Ken ran a tight ship and when his kids stayed with him on the weekend they knew what to expect – a place for everything, and everything in its place. He expected Anita and her boys to fall into place too, and be grateful for the opportunity to live with some order for a change.

Ken and his two stepsons battled constantly about the state of the house. He was at them constantly, but they just didn't seem to care. He didn't know how Anita had managed to put up with them, all these years.

Anita, trying not to fight with her husband, tried to stay out of it, but the truth was, she didn't really understand what her husband was so uptight about. The kids didn't hang up their jackets, it was true, but they were just going to put them on again the next day, so what was the big deal? But she didn't want to add to the conflict, so she kept her mouth shut.

Parenting is a process, and some days we're better at it than others.

The boys, who'd been raised in a home with loose housekeeping standards, liked it that way and were not about to change their ways for someone they saw as an interloper in their lives.

While all the shouting and yelling in this conflict is between Ken and the boys, the real problem is between Ken and Anita. They have different values around housekeeping and have each established very different expectations within their own families. They need to find some middle ground between themselves, first. Then, with all their kids, sit down and work out the family's housekeeping priorities. This will call for willing compromise from each person. Once standards are set, they need to be enforced by each parent with their own biological children.

The other troublesome issue in this scenario is that by not speaking up, Anita sold out her kids and set it up for them to dislike Ken even more. As soon as the conflict in values became obvious, she needed to work it out with Ken in private, instead of leaving her kids to take the heat.

Parents need to realize too, that although some of the conflicts in a stepfamily are related to being a stepfamily, many of the issues (sibling rivalry, parent/child friction, acting-out hurtful emotions, arguing, and so on) are common to all families and part of the business of raising teenagers. Teens will be quick to blame the remarriage for all the problems in the family, but the truth is that adolescence is often stressful for families, whatever their structure. In low moments one may be tempted to believe that if they'd never remarried they wouldn't be having problems with their kids, but that is unlikely. Teens are making the transition from child to adult and it is a stressful process. As they struggle to grow up, they experience very intense emotions and these feelings and frustrations cannot help but spill over into the family. Parents need to be patient with their teens, and patient with themselves. Parenting is a process, and some days we're better at it than others.

The behaviour that normally goes along with being a newlywed make teens exceedingly uncomfortable.

SEX IN THE FAMILY

I'm not sure why it's so, but it seems to be universally true, that teenagers desperately want to believe that their parents do not have sex. While many five-year-olds will pester their parents for the full-colour details, most fifteen-year-olds would gratefully buy into the cabbage patch theory.

The behaviour that normally goes along with being a newlywed – lingering kisses, touching, cuddling in bed all morning – make teens exceedingly uncomfortable. Kids need to witness tenderness. It's good for them to have a new role model of what marriage can be, but to help them deal with their confused feelings, parents should try to minimize displays of sexuality like lingering kisses.

Regarding the sexuality of the teens in the house, being in a stepfamily requires more thought and discussion than a nuclear family. In a nuclear family, society has imposed taboos around incest that make it very clear what is and is not acceptable and these taboos normally keep behaviour under control. Rules that may not be necessary in a nuclear family, like wearing robes over underwear, or closing bedroom doors, may be necessary in a home where family members, particularly teens, are not related by blood.

In a family meeting, everyone should talk about where their comfort and discomfort levels are and agree on house rules around issues like nudity, behaviour, and jokes. Bathroom and bedroom etiquette needs to be defined. For example, bedroom doors should be closed when someone is dressing, while bathroom doors should be locked when bathing.

Intentional sexual acting-out is also a possibility. A teen may use it as a weapon, as an attention-getting device, or in an attempt to evaluate their own sexual attractiveness.

For Example: Fourteen-year-old Stephanie, insecure about her own attractiveness and sexuality, flirts with her stepfather. Horrified, he pulls back from their relationship and, eager to prove to himself that "nothing is going on", eliminates any signs of affection from his behaviour. Hurt by this, and trying to reach him, she becomes even more flirtatious. He retreats even further and their relationship becomes hostile. Confused, Stephanie doesn't understand why her stepfather, once affectionate and loving, has turned against her. She comes to the conclusion that this rejection means she is ugly and unlovable.

The sex issue is a big one for a stepfamily with teens and there is really only one way to handle it – communication. Although discussions about sexuality and discomfort levels may be embarrassing and hard to initiate, they must be. Forming a stepfamily is basically throwing a group of strangers into an intimate situation with each other. Each person comes into this new relationship with their own family history and what may be absolutely normal behaviour to one person (such as walking around in underwear) may be perceived as a "come on" to someone else. Everyone will be much more comfortable if they have a chance to find out where each person's discomfort levels are and establish some behavioural ground rules together.

STEPFAMILIES ARE DIFFERENT

We are accustomed to basing our evaluation of the success or failure of family relationships on the nuclear family model. This model is clear about what a parent and child relationship should look like; close and loving. But nuclear families with teenagers have evolved over twelve-to-twenty years and there is a big difference, for example, between being presented with one's tiny, newborn daughter and meeting a fifteen-year-old stepdaughter for the first time. Stepparents do not instantly love their stepchildren, nor do stepchildren instantly love stepparents. Stepfamilies have to block out useless comparisons to the nuclear family model and build a stepfamily based on the people in it.

To begin with, there needs to be a neutral period of several years during which no one is expected to love each other. Respectful co-existence should be the goal. It usually takes several years just for a stepfamily to stabilize and everyone to feel comfortable with each other.

> *Stepfamilies who consider themselves solid report two things:*
> *1. affection and love develop slowly; and*
> *2. success as a family unit does not necessarily mean being emotionally close.*

Stepfamilies need to give their relationships a pleasant environment within which to grow. During those first years, especially, the biological parent must take the lead when it comes to setting limits, making rules and imposing discipline. Without trying to force a relationship the teen isn't ready for, the stepparent can look for interests and activities that will help build a positive relationship with their new stepson or daughter. Maybe it's as simple as a television sitcom they both enjoy or a card game they play after dinner. Without pushing too much (remember, teens don't usually want to hang out too much with parents – step or biological) look for bridges of mutual laughter, enjoyment, effort or interest. Admire your stepchildren. Find something, no matter how small it is, that you genuinely like about them and let them know.

Stepparents should remember as well, that adolescence is a particularly volatile and self-centred period of development. Even biological parents who have all those years of bonding and happy memories in the bank still find adolescence a challenge.

Stepparents do not instantly love their stepchildren, nor do stepchildren instantly love stepparents.

Families Have History

A stepfamily is formed with members who already have a great deal of history behind them. Values and priorities and ways of communicating with each other have developed over a very long time and are so bone-deep it is almost impossible to articulate what they are, never mind why. Even the mundane aspects of daily life are based on behaviour that we do without thinking, simply because this is the way we do it in our family:

* Do you eat fish and chips with your fingers?
* Do you fold towels in thirds and stack fold out?
* Do you roll your underwear in a ball?
* Do you eat your eggs sunny side up?
* Do you change both sheets once a week?
* Do you change your pyjamas every night?
* Do you all use the same hairbrush?

Practices that are absolutely normal in one family, may horrify another, so a great deal of patience and tolerance is required. A stepparent who comes into the family and declares, for instance, that eating fish and chips with your fingers is disgusting, is out of line. What he or she is saying will be interpreted to mean that they think the fish and chip eaters themselves are disgusting, and this remark will be seen as an assault on their family unit.

Families have history and this history needs to be respected, even in the particulars of how they conduct the everyday activities of living.

They need to talk about their different beliefs and different ways of doing things. It's usually possible for people and their differing ways to

Do you all use the same hairbrush?

coexist. For example, there is nothing wrong with four members of the family eating fish and chips with their hands while three members eat them with forks and knives. Stepparents need a very light touch when it comes to meddling in "the way we've always done it."

Celebrations and Traditions

One of the major areas of conflict is often that around major celebrations and the family traditions inherent in those celebrations. We often take it for granted that everyone does things a certain way and in those first years after a stepfamily comes together, kids will feel betrayed if sudden changes are sprung on them. The family needs to sit down, well in advance of any major celebration, and discuss what everyone's expectations are.

There may be differing expectations for example, of how birthdays should be celebrated. One family has always done so with lots of hoopla

Traditions and rituals of different families may actually collide and crash.

– a dinner party that includes grandparents, aunts, uncles and cousins, oodles of gifts, fully decorated house, and special treatment all day long. Another family is more low-key about birthdays; a birthday cheque and restaurant dinner for the immediate family only. When these families join together as a stepfamily, they do so with their own expectations of how birthdays are celebrated. If they never talk about these expectations, there is bound to be confusion and hurt feelings when birthday expectations are not met.

It's not necessary that each person's birthday be celebrated exactly the same way, but the family does need to understand what is important to each person and agree on how far the family can go toward accommodating that.

Celebration of major holidays like Christmas are often areas of intense conflict because there is so much emotion attached to having the family "together for Christmas" and the traditions and rituals of different families may actually collide and crash. One family opens gifts Christmas Eve, another on Christmas morning. One family spends Boxing Day with extended family from near and far, while another always spends Boxing Day on the ski slopes. Roast turkey is always the festive dinner for one, Baked Goose for the other; no one misses Christmas Eve Midnight Mass in one family, while the other family always spends Christmas Eve with old friends, playing Pictionary and eating fondue.

The key, again, is to sit down together as a family. Order in a pizza and give yourselves lots of time to do this. Start by having each member of the family tell how they've celebrated the holiday in the past and have them describe the rituals and traditions they most love about the season. Honour each other's memories. This is hard stuff to let go of and will probably be an emotionally-charged time. Ask each person to decide on those two or three things that mean the most to them.

For Example: Susan may say that she loves waking up Christmas morning for stollen and hot chocolate while everyone opens gifts. Ben may decide that what he loves the most is going to hear The Messiah. Carey enjoys spending time with her cousins, playing cards and eating a big turkey dinner, while Josey wouldn't want to miss Midnight Mass.

If one tried to duplicate all the traditions of both families there would be chaos, but if the family knits together a new kind of celebration, one that is based on what is most important to each person, there is a real chance that everyone will feel reasonably satisfied. If these decisions are made well in advance of the actual holiday, individuals have the time they may need to resolve any disappointments they have and can join in whole heartedly.

A NEW FAMILY

It's true, there are lots of bumps and potholes on the stepfamily road to happiness, but it is wise to remember that life is a journey, not a destination. Happiness is found along the way, in a thousand little moments that if noticed and enjoyed, add up to a lifetime. Given patience and the time they need to develop and deepen, the relationships between people in a stepfamily can be warm and wonderful and fulfilling.

Stepfamilies are no better and no worse than nuclear families, just different. They're built on their own blueprint, looking at what the individuals in them need and can give each other. The "stepfamily house" is different from the "nuclear family house" because the people in it have much more complex relationships. There needs to be room in the stepfamily house for the couple to bond and establish the strength of their relationship (in nuclear families the couple usually does this before children arrive). There needs to be a place for biological parents and their children to have time apart from the rest of the family; and time for stepparents to begin forming a relationship of trust with their stepchildren. There needs to be a place for the stepfamily to talk about finding compromises between how each family does things differently, and room for the new ways of doing things they'll establish together. There needs to be

*The "stepfamily house" is different from
the "nuclear family house" because the
people in it have much more complex
relationships.*

a place for each family's history; room for it to be respected and room for those relationships like grandchild and grandparent to flourish. There needs to be lots of space for differences and someplace safe for conflict to be worked out.

Stepfamily houses are different too, in the materials of which they're constructed. The couple is the foundation, as in nuclear families, but in the case of stepfamilies, this couple is also attached to former spouses and the disappointments, betrayals, pain and anger that those relationships engendered. The children in stepfamilies don't arrive as tiny, new babes ready to love whomever feeds and cuddles them. No, these kids arrive with attitude. They're already complex, fascinating, intensely interactive building materials. There's twice as much extended family to work with, but they're not malleable material. Some will happily fit in wherever they're most needed, but others are rigid and have to be worked around. There are positives and negatives, but mostly just more ...more people, more passion, more complexity.

A stepfamily is custom built ...by the people who are in it.

Chapter Fifteen

THE OLDER TEEN – YOUNG ADULT
Negotiating a New Relationship

Just about when you figure you have this "parenting a teen" gig figured out, you turn around and realize that you don't have an adolescent anymore, you now have another, albeit young, adult living in your house. If you've been parenting your teen more or less along the philosophical lines of this book (increasing responsibility for own decision making) you'd think this shouldn't be a major jolt.

Hah!

A Paradigm Shift

A paradigm shift needs to happen somewhere in your child's late teens or early twenties, whether you want it to or not. For most of us it's a wrench.

For Example: Mom answers the phone. It's Dr. Johnstone's office asking for her son Alex. They have "test results" for him. Test results? And who is Dr. Johnstone? Their family physician is Dr. Wong. The nurse on the phone won't give her the results so Mom, impatient and worried, waits for nineteen-year-old Alex to return home. When Alex returns he is guarded and evasive. "It's not life threatening, Mom. Just don't worry about it, okay? I'm handling it."

It is very, very difficult for a parent to back off in this kind of situation. Since that helpless little baby was placed into your arms nineteen years ago, it has been your responsibility to ensure the health, safety, and well-being of this person. Your teen has been not only your moral responsibility but your legal responsibility as well. After nineteen or so years of being pre-occupied with their well-being all of a sudden you're being told it's none of your business? Backing off when we have reason to believe there might be a problem with our child, no matter what their age, is very difficult for most of us.

After nineteen or so years of being preoccupied with their well-being all of a sudden you're being told it's none of your business?

But backing off is a decision we all have to make because, like it or not, our teen will force it. Older teens can become quite secretive about their affairs and if we hope to keep a good relationship with them during this period we must respect the natural transition that is taking place. It's what we've been working toward all their life. They are an adult, taking up the reins of their own lives, just as we always expected they would.

A few years later they'll probably ask our advice about a medical or work or relationship problem, but during this adolescent-to-adult transition their need to separate from us means they'll see our interest in them as interference. Once they've proven to themselves and the whole world that they can indeed look after themselves, they will probably be more willing to confide in us, provided, we've not been in there criticizing everything they do. If they feel that they have to defend every decision they make and hide their mistakes from us, we will blow the adult-to-adult relationship. Just think for a moment about your other adult-to-adult relationships. If your "friend" was always telling you what to do, got angry when you didn't take their advice or said "I told you so", when things didn't work out – would you want to see them? Wouldn't you avoid seeing him and when you did, keep your business to yourself?

Of course there are some aspects of the parent-child relationship that are different than friend-to-friend, but parents will go a long way toward nourishing their relationship with adult children if they keep the principles of adult friendship at the forefront.

The adolescent-to-young-adult transition doesn't happen in a straightforward continuum. It's more of a zig zag, two-steps-forward, one-step-back, kind of trip.

LIVING WITH A YOUNG ADULT

This gets very interesting. Interesting, because once a parent makes the adjustment to "I now have an adult here so I will back off and treat them like an adult", the parent thinks everything should proceed smoothly.

Hah!

The reason it doesn't, is because the adolescent-to-young-adult transition doesn't happen in a straightforward continuum. It's more of a zig zag, two-steps-forward, one-step-back, kind of trip. And there's no map. At any one time your older teen could be in "I'm an adult now, I'll handle this my own way", mode or in "But I'm your kid you're supposed to help me", mode. You won't always know right off whether you're dealing with the young adult or the late adolescent. You'll be expected to know, of course, but it can be tricky.

> *For Example: Dad asks his daughter Alicia to call if she's going to be later than twelve. Clearly indignant, Alicia informs him that she is an adult now and shouldn't have to check in like some kid. However, the next day Alicia is upset because there's no hair gel. Dad tells her that since she's now working and not going to school, he expects her to buy her own hair gel . Alicia is shocked. After all, he's the parent, isn't he? Don't parents always buy this kind of stuff? They always did before.*

Young adults can also be very moody. They've still got a great deal of developmental work to do and these can be years when they are under a lot of stress vis-a-vis the job market, post-secondary education and their love life. Their boyfriend or girlfriend may be putting them under pressure to make a commitment they're not ready for. Teens who were A-students or sports stars in high school, enter the university milieu and dis-

The "adult" behaviour will come and go for a few years, kind of like a radio station that fades in and out, getting more consistent the closer you get to the transmission tower.

cover that in the larger world they are just mediocre. Suddenly law school or a modelling contract or that great job in broadcasting are not givens. When they go on job interviews they are told to come back when they have some experience. It's a tough market out there and they are scared they don't have the right stuff to make it.

One of the major differences between maturity and youthfulness is the ability to see things in perspective. As forty- or fifty-year-old adults we know that if our teen doesn't get this job, he'll get another. If she does-n't make law school this year, she can try again next year. If this girlfriend packs up and moves away, there'll be someone who's even more right for him. In the grand scheme of things, these are not life or death matters. Disappointing yes, life threatening, no. I wouldn't suggest you be quite that blunt, however, with a hysterical twenty-one-year-old who has just had her entrance application rejected. Realize that they simply aren't looking at things through the same lens you are. It's very important that as parents we don't trivialize our teens' concerns because doing so is a major block to communication. You might be thinking to yourself, "That's no big deal, what's she so uptight about", but don't say it. That doesn't mean you have to lie, you could simply say something like, "I can see how upset you are. Can I help you brainstorm some options?"

There are lots of reasons for teens to be uptight, tense, and stressed out at this time in their lives. That doesn't mean you shouldn't insist on respectful behaviour in your home, but at times you may need to cut them a little more slack. The "adult" behaviour will come and go for a few years, kind of like a radio station that fades in and out, getting more con-sistent the closer you get to the transmission tower. Your young adult really will turn into a full-time adult, but it doesn't happen because they reach a certain birthday. Be prepared for your new adult's behaviour to regress at times.

You might think this regression would take your young adult back to say, age fifteen. But when they are especially uptight or tense, expect them to regress all the way to age two. Honest. Looking at a full-grown (often much taller) son or daughter, we make the mistake of thinking we really are dealing with another adult, so it's very easy to get sucked into returning the screaming and yelling with screaming and yelling. But remember, you are the bonafide adult and you need to act like one. Try to remember that the more regressive a young adult acts, the more they need us to behave like the grown-up.

The late-adolescent to young-adult years are a training ground for learning the skills they will need for their own adult-to-adult relationship with a partner some day.

For Example: Josh, under a lot of stress to get good marks on his mid-terms treated his mom with rudeness and insensitivity. He later apologized, explaining that he only behaved this way because he was under so much stress. "I know I'm a jerk sometimes, but I just can't help it." His mother explained that if this was so, it was lucky he still lived in his family home where a great deal would be forgiven. Had he treated a wife the same way he treated his mother, stress or no stress, he would have had a marriage in trouble. She suggested that, since stress would always be something he should expect to crop up in his life, he use the next few years at home to learn how to handle stress in a way that did not mean he had to be rude others. "Look on this as a training ground for marriage," she said.

Modify Expectations

Young adults often have incredibly busy lives. Between work, college, socializing, fitness, and their passions like rock climbing, music, mountain biking, dancing, skiing, or whatever, there is very little time for family. Although we remain important anchors, the early-adult years are a time when their family relationships have to be taken on faith.

Whenever I was having a "heart-to-heart" discussion with one of my sons about doing their share of the housekeeping chores, I often had a fantasy running of how, if they were in a room-mate situation, the room-mate wouldn't put up with their lack of participation and they'd have some real life lessons about what it takes to keep a household running. But when I'm honest with myself I remember that most of the room-

Although we remain important anchors, the early-adult years are a time when their family relationships have to be taken on faith.

mates I had at their age, were not very tidy. I even remember, in my own case, coming back from a vacation to discover that I'd forgotten to wash up my dishes before I left. I was therefore now sharing my suite with another life form. Cleaning wasn't something any of us ever did unless we were going to have a party. Even then, maybe not.

The point is, young adulthood is not a time when housekeeping has any kind of priority with most teens. They are far too busy living and working and trying to pull decent marks. As one of my own sons put it, "It's not as if I were laying around watching television all the time. I just don't have time to keep up the housekeeping. It's at the bottom of my list of things to do." And I had to agree. There wasn't anything in his life that I wanted him to drop so he could vacuum more. Parents may find that this period, when their kids are so busy, is a time to lighten up on their expectations of them. If it's at all possible, look at your home in terms of making modifications that would give each of you more independence, something that would more clearly demarcate their space and your space. Could you finish a room in the basement? Make a suite in the garage? Make an "outside" door to their room? These kinds of modifications can relieve a lot of the tension that arises when young adult children continue living at home.

This is also a time in their lives when family events and activities, from every-night dinner to Grandpa's sixty-fifth birthday party, will have a low priority with them. I don't think it's that these things cease to matter to them, it's just that there are so many other *more* pressing things to do. Of course we can prevail upon their sense of what's the right and decent thing to do (such as attending Grandpa's sixty-fifth birthday) but we can't pull that one out of the bag too often or it loses its power to influence them. I remember feeling quite sad the first few times I went off to a family event without my oldest son. I also felt sad the first time we took a holiday without him. Heck, I cried buckets the first day I left him in daycare and went to work for five hours! These are all separations on a path that we know is taking them away from us and they tug at the heart something fierce. But the thing is, our kids have to set their own priorities and if we can stay low-key about it, they are more likely to willingly and happily attend family events because they are important to *them*.

One of the things I most missed as my sons turned into young adults, was their nightly appearance at the dinner table. I really enjoyed hearing about everyone's day, applauding the triumphs and commiserating over the disasters. But between school, training programs, part-time jobs, girlfriends and their social life, my husband and I found ourselves, more often than not, staring at each other over the salt and pepper shakers. This is reality. Hanging around waiting for their parents to get home so they can eat dinner together every night is just not as important as getting on with their evening. I can understand that.

Look at your home in terms of making modifications that would give each of you more independence.

At the same time, it's important that family life doesn't go completely by the boards. Keep having family council meetings, perhaps more infrequently, but at least once a month sit down together and work out any outstanding issues and plan for the future together. Plan to spend some time together, just the family, every month – movie night, biking, playing cards, skiing, going to a concert, or whatever you would all enjoy. Your times together may not be as frequent as they were when your kids were younger, but be intentional about keeping your family relationships strong and loving.

BOOMERANG KIDS

These are the young adults who move out, live on their own for a time, then return to the family home, sometimes with a child in tow. This happens for a lot of reasons, a few of which are:
- their love life is on the rocks and they need us;
- the good job they thought was secure isn't, and they can't afford to live on their own while they look for a new one;

- return to school;
- physical or mental illness; or
- once they're out there paying their own bills they realize how little their pay cheques actually buy and want to return to the family home where they have a better standard of living.

For parents who've come to enjoy the freedom (and financial bene-fits) of a child-free lifestyle, this return to the family nest can be disruptive. At first they open their arms in welcome, but as the months pass this welcome can turn into resentment. When there are still other teens at home, the real estate was no doubt re-arranged when the boomeranger first left, so these younger siblings will resist going back to the way things were. And perhaps that's the secret to making boomerang situations work. We never can return to the way things were. We have to start with the way things are.

> ## *We never can return to the way things were. We have to start with the way things are.*

Examine Your Attitude

The return of an adult child can sometimes make parents feel like fail-ures. After all, we raised this young adult, prepared them for the world and now it may look like they can't cut it out there. Obviously we didn't do such a great job of raising them after all.

Boomerang kids are usually disappointed in themselves as well. They haven't been able to make it on their own and this can be a real blow to their self esteem. The worst thing a parent can do in this case is to "make it all better" because that just confirms to everyone that Jed or Janice is a failure who can't make it on their own without Mom or Dad.

Instead of regarding your adult child as a dependant who needs to be taken care of, treat them as the young adult they are. They are struggling and may need some help from you, but they are, nevertheless, an adult. When they learned how to ride a bike, they fell off a few times and even after they got that bike up and rolling, it was pretty wobbly for awhile. Then one day you looked out the window to see them screaming down the street, "no hands".

We all conquer life's milestones at our own, individual pace. One of

Leaving home is just another milestone,
and some kids need several tries at it before
they're steady enough for full independence.

my sons learned to walk at nine months, the other not until he was thirteen months. But the early walker was much more timid about being away from home and didn't do any "away camps" until he was fourteen. The late walker eagerly tore off to week-long Cub camps at age eight, much earlier than his Mom was ready for! Leaving home is just another milestone, and some kids need several tries at it before they're steady enough for full independence.

How Can I Help Them?

To get your adult child ready for their next attempt at independence, parents need to duplicate the real world as much as possible. We need to have the same expectations of our adult child as the world outside does. Some of these expectations are that they will:

- *take responsibility for their own needs such as sleep, nutrition, clothing, health care, personal products, etc.*
- *not do things in our home that we are uncomfortable with*
- *solve their own personal problems*
- *be respectful of other's needs*
- *respect our privacy*
- *commit themselves either to education or to searching for a job capable of supporting themselves*
- *manage their own finances including paying a share of their earnings toward the upkeep of the household*

Sometimes a list of expectations like this is easier to read than it is to put into practice. What it means to our day-to-day relationship is that we don't get sucked into the parent-child syndrome in which we tell them when to cut their hair, approve or disapprove of their friends, and nag

*Parents do not have the right to say with whom their adult
child has sex, but they do have the right to say whether that
will happen under their roof.*

them to clean up their room. This behaviour is as inappropriate with
them as it would be with any other adult. Parents must respect their adult
children's right to make decisions about their own lives. The following
areas, for example, would be off limits to parents:

- *what they eat*
- *when they sleep*
- *their appearance*
- *who their friends are*
- *who their lovers are*
- *where they work*
- *how they spend their money*

That said, however, parents have the right to determine what happens in their own home. For example, parents do not have the right to say with whom their adult child has sex, but they do have the right to say whether that will happen under their roof.

The non-negotiable bottom line for living together is the simple fact that it is the parent's home so the parent gets to make the rules. The young adult may not like this and may long for the day when they have their own place again where they can do whatever they want. That's as it should be.

Fitting In

Adult children who return home will probably find that things have changed while they've been gone. A sibling may have moved into their old room; their rehearsal garage may now be a pottery studio. Little sister may now have custody of the old car and an exchange student might be living in the extra bedroom. Mom may have gotten a job or Dad may have retired. It's important for the boomeranger (who is only home temporarily, after all) to adapt to the new order of things. Other family members should not be put out because they've returned.

Support in a Crisis

Adult children sometimes return home because they are in a state of crisis. They are not capable of coping with the world out there, so Mom and Dad open their arms wide to take in and comfort their wounded one. This is crisis support. It's important that we be there to give it; that's what families are for. But it's equally important that we don't linger there. Adult children need to be respected for being adults. As they start to regain strength, we need to increase our expectations of them. Ask them to fold laundry or prepare a simple meal. Expect them to start doing whatever they are capable of doing. They need to re-build their self esteem and they can only do that if they start feeling capable again.

Addictions and Abuse

Adult children addicted to alcohol, other drugs, or an unsavoury lifestyle often try to return home. Their parents, hearts full of love and pain, struggle again and again to rescue them. But if we allow them to live at home without enrolling in a drug treatment program or taking any visible action to turn their lives around, we are supporting them in their addiction.

When do you throw them out?

Only the parent involved can answer this, but a good guideline is the following:

When you believe that you have done everything possible to convince them to get help or when you have reached your own personal limit of what you can tolerate, they need to go.

Remember that closing the door to your home does not close the door to your heart. Ask for information at whatever agency in your area handles alcohol and drug education and join a support group of parents with issues similar to yours (an addicted son or daughter, for example). These people can be a great source of support and information.

Living With Adult Children Can Be Great

With all the cautions to "put it in writing" and so on, one might come to the conclusion that living with adult children is fraught with problems. That's not necessarily true. Many people report that these arrangements work out just fine for them. There can be huge advantages for everyone. Parents get someone they know and trust as a "tenant"; kids get economical accommodation while they go to school, save for a house, etc.; grandparents and grandchildren have the opportunity to truly share their lives; and so on. These happy situations do not usually happen, however, simply because the parties had good intentions. They happen because the parties involved sat down and talked out issues while they were still in the realm of the theoretical, before there were any emotions attached.

Writing a Contract

Many parents and their adult children find that talking through all the issues, then putting their agreement into writing is very helpful. Some of the components of that contract might be:

1. Time Frame

   Agree on a time frame, after which the adult child will move out or the contract will be re-negotiated.

2. Rent or Services

   If the young adult cannot pay rent, determine what they will do in lieu of it – cooking, cleaning, chauffeuring, repairs, gardening, car maintenance, or laundry are examples. What will happen once they do get a job?

3. Meals

   Who shops, pays for, cooks, and cleans up the meals?

4. Household Chores

   Draw up a list of all the jobs that need to be done and take turns choosing from the list until all the jobs are equitably distributed.

5. Telephone, Stereo, Television, Computer, and Tools

   What are the conditions for using these? What happens when things need repair?

6. Guests

   When, how many, how late, overnight, where will they sleep?

7. Vehicles

   Can they use your vehicle? Who will pay for gas, insurance, repairs?

8. Children

   Who has primary responsibility for the child/ren? Under what conditions will grandparents care for child/ren? Who pays for child/ren's special needs? Where may child/ren play? How (and who) will discipline child/ren?

9. Addictions

   What visible action will they be taking to turn their lives around?

PARENTS ...We Need Them Always

At this point I struggle for an analogy that accurately portrays the role that parents play in their young (and not so young) adult's lives. I've often heard parents described as "anchors" and that sounds good at first – a form of security in the storms of life. But an anchor is also a tether and you can only move so far before your boat is hauled up short. I don't think anchor describes the kind of parent I want to be.

As parents we're often described as "roots." I have some problems with that too because if you separate the plant from its roots it dies very quickly. I would like to think that if I weren't here my kids would do just fine. That is, after all, what I've been preparing them for.

What it comes down to, for me, is that parents are just that, "parents." In those first few months we are their whole world. A few years later we're still very important but they now know that they can get a great deal of what they need from other people too. Their world has expanded. During adolescence they learn how to take care of themselves, how to make the decisions that will keep them safe and healthy. For a few years, then, our older teens and young adults struggle with the necessity to separate from us, to truly establish their own identities and values systems. During these years it sometimes looks like they really don't need us. Don't believe it. Even as older adults we need our parents. They provide us with a set of givens that make our world more secure. I'm 100% certain that I won't ever return home to live with my parents (and my parent's home is now an apartment in a senior's complex, not the acreage they lived on when I left home) but, believing that I could, that they would never turn me away, is an enduring thread in my personal security blanket. I also have faith that no matter what I do they will always love me. Partners have been known to come and go and kids get pre-occupied with their own lives, but my parents – they will always love me and always be thrilled to see me.

My parents are getting older and their health isn't great these days. I wouldn't dream, anymore, of burdening them with problems that they cannot solve for me. But sometimes, in the middle of a day when it seems like the whole world is beating up on me, I'll call them up just to hear the sound of their voices. They are an oasis in the midst of craziness. For a few moments, courtesy of technology, I am transported to a place where

I am the smartest, prettiest, most loved person on the face of the earth. They have absolutely no objectivity about me. I am simply the best, and that comes through loud and clear. The world that was out of kilter just a few moments before gets plunked back onto its axis and I am empowered, once again, to slay dragons. My Mom and Dad love me. They think I'm the best. That love and belief in will be a sustaining truth in my life, even when they are no longer alive.

We need our parents........always.

We need our parents........always.

RECOMMENDED RESOURCES

Active Parenting of Teens
Michael H. Popkin   Active Parenting Press, Atlanta, GA   1997

This is a very good video-based parenting program. Ask if your local family services agency or university extension department have it in their library. < www.cadvision.com/alreynar/ >

Changing Bodies, Changing Lives
Ruth Bell   Times Books   1998

This is an excellent manual to the adolescent mind and body: sexual development; relationships; birth control; pregnancy; abortion; becoming a parent; STD's; drugs and alcohol; depression and suicide; and taking care of ones self. Every home with an adolescent should have a copy of this book – information and insight for both teens and their parents.

Choices and Consequences
What To Do When a Teenager Uses Alcohol/Drugs
Dick Schaefer   Johnson Institute Books, Minneapolis, MN   1996

An excellent resource for parents dealing with teens who have alcohol/drug problems. It offers detection and intervention strategies, as well as lots of support. Contact the Johnstone Institute at 7205 Ohms Lane, Minneapolis, MN 55439-2159, 1-800-231-5165

Divorce and New Beginnings
Genevieve Clapp, Ph.D.   John Wiley & Sons, Inc.   1992

This is a comprehensive guide to weathering divorce, then rebuilding your life. It's a practical and useful resource for recovery – for parents and their children.

How to Deal With Your Acting-Up Teenager
Robert T. and Jean Bayard   M. Evans & Co., Inc.   1986

Parents who are having serious problems with their kids must get this book. It proscribes a philosophy for dealing with troubled teens that tackles the biggies like stealing, alcohol/drug abuse, promiscuity, lying, running away, and so on. Parents who don't have kids with these problems will also benefit from this book. Implementing the underlying philosophy will go a long way towards ensuring these problem areas don't develop.

PFLAG - Parents, Families, and Friends of Lesbians and Gays
website: <www.pflag.ca>

This website offers parents, families, and friends of lesbians and gays information, education, and resources to help them understand and support their gay and lesbian family members.

Parents Together
website: <*www.online.com/parents*>

This is a self-help parent support group for parents of troubled teens. This site is worth a visit because it offers an excellent model for such support groups.

Please Listen to Me:
Your Guide to Understanding Teenagers and Suicide
Marion Crook   Self-Counsel Press   1992

This insightful resource is the result of the many interviews Marion has done with suicide-prone teens. Read what your kids would tell you if they could and learn what you as a parent can do to make it much less likely that your teen will consider suicide as an option for solving their problems. Contact Self-Counsel Press at: 1481 Charlotte, North Vancouver, B.C. Canada, V7J 1H1

Speaking of Sex
Meg Hickling, RN   Northstone Press   1999

This isn't a book about teenage sexuality per se, but Meg has a great way of making parents and kids so comfortable with talking about sex that it applies across all ages. We all learn something from Meg and after a lifetime as a sexual health educator, she has hundreds of humorous stories that make the learning more fun.

The Plugged In Parent
Steve Bennett   Times Books, Random House   1998

This book is an excellent resource for parents concerned about the effects of the computer and the internet in their home. It starts from the premise that the reader knows nothing - and helps them choose the technology that best suit their family's needs. The author then continues on to teach parents how to make the computer and internet connection an asset in their children's lives.

The Weekend Parent: Learning to Live Without Full-time Kids
Carolyn Pogue   Western Producer Prairie Books   1990

A supportive resource for helping parents without full-time custody of their kids rebuild their lives with this new reality. It promotes the concept that a parent is always a parent and their kids will always need them.

What Colour Is My Parachute
Richard Nelson Bolles   Ten Speed Press   2000

This constantly updated resource for job-hunters is a practical manual for helping anyone, parent or teen, explore which careers and job placements would be the best fit for them.

Index